Patriot Call

Of

Ron Paul

Don White

A short version of Ron Paul's

Liberty Defined

Copyright 2012

Printed by Create Space Charleston, SC

CONTENTS

Patriot Call

Of

Ron Paul

Don White

Short Version, Congressman Paul's

Liberty Defined, Copyright 2012

Printed by Create Space Charleston, SC

Introduction

I write to all Americans—

Republicans and Democrats alike

Today, something akin to the retirement of George Washington could occur. Texas Congressman Ron Paul, the most conservative man in the House of Representatives, soon will retire from politics. That is if he loses his bid to become president of the United States.

Let us make sure he wins. Dr. Paul is the most intelligent and patriotic candidate of all. We would miss him dearly if he follows through with his retirement announcement.

For many, this would not be a tragedy. But if you are a libertarian you are saying *What a shame!* Tea Party conservatives would lament because Ron Paul's ideas provided most of the nation-saving insight for that movement, not including their apparent love of preemptive war.

But Let us save America!

The intention of Ron Paul was to follow George Washington and Thomas Jefferson. They suggested that one should serve in Washington for a short time and return home to assume an original profession.

Dr. Ron Paul did not want to stay 24 years. In fact, he was the first Congressman in America to write a bill proposing term limits and that was in the 1970s. He proposed term limits multiple times during his self-interrupted twelve-term service to his country.

His term limit bill was always defeated, so when he saw that people in Washington would not budge on their moderate and liberal ideas he decided to stay and fight.

Freedom-loving people across this great nation are glad he did. Congressman Paul knew he could make a difference and he has. What would America be like without conservatives like Ron Paul in the House of Representatives?

When democrats heard that Congressman Paul was retiring they were ecstatic. Their minds sent up victory balloons and rockets. They were glad this feisty medical doctor-lawmaker would no longer be on the scene writing books and pestering the liberals with sound thinking on a variety of issues, all opposing progressive demagogy and big government.

This is the same Ron Paul who ran for president as a libertarian in 2008, a man who is again running for president in 2012 as a republican.

Luke warm critics might say that if the past is any indication of the future, he can't win in 2012. Nonsense! He wasn't supposed to win in his first bid for the House of Representatives, either, when he ousted a democrat incumbent.

Something told me to offer Ron Paul my help, but how? By reducing his latest book down to the nuts and bolts of what he believes and entice those "kids" who didn't know any better last time to read and understand Ron Paul's glorious ideas. Then I hope they will believe and take action at the polls.

America's youth and old alike need to hear Congressman Paul's message—that what America needs most right now is fewer, not more, rules, which make it almost impossible to run a small business. Seventy percent of new jobs in America today are created by small businesses, but we have chained them with rules and regulations that make it almost impossible for them to compete with foreign countries.

The goal is to reduce the size of government and win those jobs back. Ron Paul can fix that. He would spend less and balance our budgets; cut government fraud and waste and stop those senseless wars.

This is part of Ron Paul's program. He *can* fix America, fortifying us economically, socially, and militarily with real clear conservative values that will liberate the nation from the heavy yoke of big government and years and years of wars of aggression that God warns will lead to our downfall.

Ron Paul is a moral man. He has decided to retire from the U.S. House of Representatives after 12 terms so that he can concentrate all of his efforts on winning the Republican nomination for president. That's the good news.

However, if he fails to win the presidency, his leaving the House of Representatives becomes a tragedy. It would be hard to think of an America without Ron Paul to lead the way. It isn't a happy prospect—depriving a nation of his wisdom, his brilliant mind, and his ability to see behind the rhetoric what needs to be done to set this country on a true, free, and successful course.

Ron Paul is a highly educated and intelligent common-sense man whom I, a former Democrat (almost 50 years ago) and supporter of "big tent" moderates like Mitt Romney, now vow to back.

What was I thinking? I should have gone full tilt in support of Ron Paul much earlier. When you finish reading this book, I hope you are having similar thoughts.

If it took me a while to see the light, there must be plenty more out there like me that need re-educating on Ron Paul. I am convinced that *Patriot Call Of Ron Paul*, my short version of his book *Liberty Defined*, is just what will do that.

Somewhat like conservative Senator Barry Goldwater (R-AZ) before him, Congressman. Paul's a great communicator because he has the facts and tells the truth. Not so with Obama.

As a public speaker, Obama often falls flat, especially without his teleprompter, but his personal charm and charisma have so far saved him. Well, America, that's about to end.

"If you love me pass my bill?"

Obama wrote and said those stupid lines? What has he done to warrant our love? Just the opposite is true. He hates America so he deserves our scorn. He has done everything he could to bring America down. He shames America in front of foreign governments. He is not a cheerleader for America's exception-alism or Yankee inventiveness. Quite the contrary. Frankly, he is a public embarrassment to both Democrats and Republicans alike.

Last January I said that I wouldn't be surprised to hear he will not seek a second term. But, alas, his pride runs over. He is not only seeking a second term, but he is attempting to change history so that a bunch of falsehoods amounts to truth. For example, the economy is in robust shape. Jobs are coming back. We're on the rebound. Nothing bad has occurred that some more Keynesian economics—more bailouts—can's solve. It is actually better for Republicans that he run because he is eminently beatable.

Obama's message is flawed and no amount of jokes, lies, and big-tooth smiles should make honest Americans believe we are better off today than we were at the end of 2008.

And what about those other two so-called orators, FDR and Woodrow Wilson? FDR gave us bigger government and the welfare state and Wilson gave us the progressive income tax, the Federal Reserve System, and broken promises that took America into World War I.

The Fed and Obama's profligate spending has just about wiped out the country's prosperity and any chance soon of escaping the economic chaos it created. But there Ben Bernanke is again—offering to fix things with another $660 Billion when everyone knows big spending has failed in the past and almost totaled out our dollar.

Our only hope is to defeat Obama at the polls with Ron Paul, the only candidate who understands the Fed—a man who promises to end the Fed and its global power nonsense. Ron Paul's mantra also includes bringing home our troops—not "all but 3,000 of them," as Obama announced, but ALL of them—cutting the spending, balancing the budget, wiping out the communist rules and regulations that stymie new business and job growth, and winning back our place as the most free country in the world.

Today, thanks to Obama and his liberal friends in Washington, America is behind socialistic Canada—in ninth place on the Heritage Foundation's list of free nations.

That's atrocious! What happened to "The Land of the Free?"

No one can tell me that having a bunch of communists and socialists in the White House writing onerous rules is good for the economic and the spiritual health of our nation.

On the political trail, at times Ron Paul may struggle with "big-tent" crowd appeal. That's because he tells it like it is. That's why liberals hate him. But Americans loved four other men who spoke their minds, Republicans Ronald Reagan and Barry Goldwater, Democrat Harry Truman and Republican Abraham Lincoln.

Could they love Paul, too? Of course, many already do. Not that Congressman Paul couldn't get even hard core Democrats to love him if he wanted. But to do so he would have to be all things to all people—and he's just too honest to be all over the board in his convictions.

One liberal moaned about Paul's delivery, "You think you're listening to Gomer Pyle." He was referring to Dr. Paul's bubbly, gentle, rural auto mechanic panache. Home folks love that style, but he gains less affection from non-libertarians. The Gomer Pyle TV persona was portrayed by popular American singer/television actor Jim Nabors, who was beloved by all in the fifties and sixties.

Today, voters are attracted to glitz and pseudo intellectualism with occasional lies and jokes to cover the untruths. The ready comeback was one of Ronald Reagan's secrets of success, but as with Paul, we trusted him because he was an honest man.

Some people prefer young, tall and handsome presidential timber with a clearly resonating voice, despite the fact those candidates have a nasty habit of over-promising and rarely delivering.

It happens all the time. When we elect a dishonest person we wake up some fine morning to find that he or she has ghosts in closets that can't be fixed with timely quips.

We deserve whom we get. Dishonesty seems today to be one of the chief shortcomings of winning White House candidates, but that's not Ron Paul.

Paul may seem somewhat verbose; at times his lines may even lack punch and wit, at least from a Madison Avenue point of view. It is because this is not Ronald Reagan at the podium, nor would Dr. Paul like to be. He's Ron Paul, a brilliant, plain and simple, tell-it-as-it-is man.

He really "brought it" before large straw poll crowds recently during his campaign for president.

If you want to get that heart-throbbing—but hollow— temporary feeling, vote for Mitt, Michelle, or Rick. That kind of yelling-whip-them-into-a-frenzy talk from candidates is cheap and insincere and it panders to emotions, not intellect.

But if you want it like it is, with earthy honesty, you had better choose Ron Paul. This man is the most intelligent and literate candidate from either party. He is the only candidate that can release us from the "big Washington" malaise America has suffered under for the past six decades.

The tragedy is that so few bother to find out what Ron Paul stands for. I wrote the short *Patriot Call From Ron Paul* version of *Liberty Defined* to help remedy that.

I was tempted to call the book *Liberty Defined For Dummies* but that title has too many negative connotations and those who read and accept it are the most intelligent Americans around, not

dummies.

The title of Congressman Paul's *New York Times* number one bestseller is *Liberty Defined, 50 Essential Issues That Affect Our Freedom.*

Liberty Defined is Paul's eighth book. What other presidential candidate has written so well, so prolifically? I also whole-heartedly endorse Congressman Paul's other books that I have read, especially *End The Fed.*

According to University of Georgia political scientist Keith Poole, Ron Paul had the most conservative voting record of any member of Congress since 1937. Move over Mr. Gingrich, Mr. Obfuscation, you are not even a conservative compared to my man Congressman Paul. His son Rand Paul was elected to the United States Senate from Kentucky in 2011, making the elder Paul the first Representative in history to serve concurrently with his son.

Dr. Paul gained prominence for his positions on many political issues, often clashing with both GOP and Democratic party leaders. He has been called the "intellectual godfather" of the Tea Party movement. In my home—and hopefully yours—we call him the best qualified candidate, the next president of the United States.

1

Abortion

Ron Paul: Some people believe that

being pro-choice is being

on the side of freedom

"I have never understood how an act of violence, killing a human being, albeit a small one in a special place, is   portrayed as a special right. To speak only of the mother's cost in carrying a baby to term ignores all thoughts of   any legal rights of the unborn.

"I believe that the moral consequences of cavalierly accepting abortion, which is the killing [or ending] of a human being's life, diminishes the value of all life."

This clear and unmistakable declaration of Ron Paul follows an incident   that occurred early in his medical career as an OB/GYN resident visiting "a surgical suite." This was in the 1960s even before abortions were legalized in America. He witnessed something he could never forget which would forever set his heart and mind against abortion.

He watched the abortion of a fetus weighing about two pounds. "It was placed in a bucket crying and struggling to breathe, and the medical personnel pretended not to notice." Soon the crying stopped and the memory of this "horrifying" event burned a singularly deep mark into Dr. Paul's heart.

Dr. Paul gives medical orders to all of us, especially to pro-life MDs and medical personnel.

1) No abortions for convenience or social reasons.

2) Never be an agent for active euthanasia.

3) Never be a participant in any manner—directly or indirectly—in torture.

4) No human experimentation. He said he wasn't referring to new drug testing with patient consent. He was referring to America's long history of military participation in human experimentation. One example was the deliberate

mistreatment of black soldiers who had syphilis called the Tuskegee   experiment.

5) Do not be involved with the state in executing criminals or in any way approving the carrying out of the death penalty.

6) Refuse to participate in government programs in which medical care is rationed for economic or social reasons that place relative value on life.

7) Do not give political or philosophical support for wars of aggression, referred to as preventive wars.

Paul, Ron. 1973, Abortion and Liberty. Lake Jackson: Foundation for Rational Economics and Education.

2

Assassination

After 9/11 President George Bush

forced on us the Patriot Act...

Barak Obama jumped on the bandwagon of scare tactics by introducing intrusive airport scanning and frisking our bodies. Now with the War Defense Appropriations Act (WDAA), the military is authorized to show up at your door and haul you, an American citizen, off to a foreign jail without due process of law—without charging you with a crime, providing you a defense attorney, and ensuring there is a trial by your peers to determine guilt. They can hold you indefinitely.

The other minor detail I want to mention is that now the president has authority to kill American citizens without due process of law. He has already killed two—one was Anwar al-Awlaki, also spelled al-Aulaqi; ArabicArabic *Anwar al-'Awlaqī*; April 21, 1971 – September 30, 2011).

He was a Yemeni American imamwho was an engineer and educator by training. According to U.S. government officials, he was a senior talent recruiter and motivator involved with planning operations for the Islamist militant group Al-Qaeda. Also his friend, a citizen who was born in Denver, Colorado, was killed in the same attack, which was ambush by drone In Yemini.

America can do better than this. If we insist on going after enemy combatants with drones, we should consider upgrading their kills by retrofitting to the drones to include loud speakers and recording equipment to warn the target that a drone is about to fly over and the target is about to expire, reading the evidence, stating that this recording is in lieu of any trial the person is entitled to under the U.S. Constitution and that he has been found guilty.

"Sorry, the bombs will drop now and if you try to run away we will kill all of your relatives and everyone else within two hundred yards of your house". This is of course a feckless, inappropriate, attempt to say there is an unlawful way for the government to look constitutional in all of this, but as you can see it would take a lot of prevarication, dissembling, deceit and twisting of the Constitution to pull this off.

Oh well, we know all of the above verbiage fitly matches the perpetrators of military assassinations and that none of the warnings and legalese would take place anyway in fear that the suspect would escape before the bombs hit the ground.

Saying they discovered in his house his blog, a Facebook page, and many YouTubeYouTube videos, the CIA, NSA, and America's military would like you to believe that the man they killed in a rather large walled Afghanistan home whom they hastily buried at sea without neutral verification was the real Osama bin Laden. This author's feeling was that this was a put-up job to bolster support for similar hit-and-run ops in Afghanistan and elsewhere or as a cover for continuing this undeclared war with a third-world nation. Many Americans are convinced it was all a lie, that the real bin Laden died of natural causes (kidney failure) ten years or more before. But as an offering of authenticity, the US government used as proof specious quotes from an unreliable Saudi news station Al Arabiya statomg that this was the "bin Laden of the Internet." The CIA does marvelous things with bribe money.

Even so, even this "bin-Laden" deserved a fair trial where the CIA would have to prove that he was, in fact, the master=mind of 9/11 and similar terrorist hits on Western targets. Even the worst Nazi World War II killers were given trials before they were convicted, sentenced, and killed. For some reason, the Barak Obama Administration has given orders to kill U.S. citizens without such amenities as habeas corpus—or should we be accurate and say, without living up to the Constitution of the United States which mandates a fair trial before any punishment is rendered.

The situation is similar with al-Awlaki, except even worse. He was an American citizen. This man, al-Awlaki and his friend had duel citizenship—Yemini and American—and nothing had been proven in a court of law that these men were even terrorists or had ever killed anyone.

So far the government has announced just these two US citizens that they have indiscriminately killed. Just two that we are aware of, but there could be dozens more unannounced assassinations.

If that sends a chill down your back, you are not alone. Our government has become so fearful of another terrorist attack—or so they would like you to believe—that the US is also moving toward allowing acceptance of assassinations of American citizens as necessary to provide national security.

Congressman Paul believes this demonstrates that we are no longer a nation of laws, but people who operate outside the law without restraint.

He believes it is a result of U.S. foreign policy gone wrong—positions that foster worldwide intervention and occupations. This has resulted in our own people becoming fearful of supposed enemies, a fear that has taught our people to allow policies they otherwise would have rebelled against.

Sixty years ago, George Orwell, author of Nineteen Eighty-Four, correctly described shocking conditions under which we in America and Great Britain are living today. This has come about in our day because leaders intentionally over-react to terrorist attacks. Many Americans are cowering into acceptance of these anti-terrorist government mandates, much to the delight of our leaders.

On 21 October 1949, writer Aldous Huxley wrote to congratulate Orwell on how fine and how profoundly important the book is. In his letter to Orwell, he predicted: "Within the next generation I believe that the world's leaders will discover that infant conditioning and narco-hypnosis are more efficient, as instruments of government, than clubs and prisons, and that the lust for power can be just as completely satisfied by suggesting people into loving their servitude as by flogging them and kicking them into obedience."

If we are fearful enough, we are willing to tolerate what otherwise might be regarded as an immoral means of dealing with the enemy, said Dr. Paul.

He posits that the use of torture to combat evildoers has been accepted by a large number of otherwise reasonable Americans as a result of those who purposefully, successfully used fear as a tactic to achieve their mischievous goals.

The war on terror is worldwide, supposedly justifying its perpetuation anywhere on the earth. "In wartime, the government assumes greater emergency powers to make secret arrests, build secret prisons, torture, and use secret rendition, allowing other more ruthless countries to do our dirty work."

Paul believes that the "war on terror" is a cliché. It is like the wars on poverty, drugs, and illiteracy. But its use is deliberate, even in these symbolic images, to con the people into believing that all citizens must cooperate and sacrifice their liberties to win the war.

This is crucial, they say, to keep our country safe. Dr. Paul believes we have forgotten that threats to the Constitution come both from without and from within.

It appears that many people in government want us to believe that the greater danger is coming from people like the underwear bomber rather than from our own government.

For years America has been involved in regime change around the world, which includes the use of assassination. But up until February 3, 2010, there was no admission to such a policy or recognition of its illegality.

On that date before the House Intelligence Committee, Director of National Intelligence Dennis Blair (DNI) admitted that this policy existed. He said being a U.S. citizen will not spare an American from getting assassinated by military or intelligence operatives.

Government argues that only a few people are assassinated, or taken out, without regard to habeas corpus or due process of law.

Yes, but just hope that you are not on their list.

You now know from the above explanation that under the Obama Administration, Americans became subject to break-in to their homes and arrest without cause the first year of his administration and to be taken to a foreign country for trial, if by the international organization called Interpol. Obama wrote the executive order himself. Now with passage of the new NDAA law, he has further authenticated his intentions and power to kill any American he wants. He is now the most ruthless and powerful man in the world. Whatever happened to our second amendment rights?

Proponents of extermination without habeas corpus say it is usually just a few that are unduly arrested and/or killed. But then it escalates as Hitler's war on the Jews did, resulting in more than four million deaths. Among many other of Hitler's prisons, Jews were killed at Auschwitz-Birkenau, a German Nazi Concentration and Extermination Camp in Poland 1940–1945. This was the largest of Hitler's death camps that housed the Jews.

"Tyranny always begins with oppression of unpopular minorities," says Paul. "Who would have ever believed that we could fall so far? The basic principle of the writ of habeas corpus has been around for 800 years, and so has the right not to be cast into indefinite detention without charges."

He said the justification for such abuse of the rule of law is all based on concocted fear by false claims associated with a lack of respect and understanding of what liberty is all about.

On September 12, 2011 at the Tampa Tea Party Express Republican debate, America was exposed to the lack of knowledge on the part of candidates and citizens alike when Ron Paul tried to explain his misunderstood, misquoted statement in his book that America caused 9/11.

It was taken out of context by TV announcer Wolf Blitzer who should know better. But he wanted to build controversy and drama because he wanted other candidates frothing at the mouth, jumping on it like hungry tigers strangling their prey. Blitz somewhat succeeded. Was it unfair? Of course it was.

When will TV syndicates dedicate themselves to correctly educating the masses rather than jumping in as part of the problem, creating and expanding on propaganda and half-truths as they do? Shame on you Mr. Blitzer.

What is the justification for anyone getting on the government's assassination list?

That person merely has to be, according to Dennis Blair, declared a "threat." No charges of a crime or plan to commit a crime are needed.

Congressman Paul said that being a threat is a purely subjective term and is morally ambiguous. Casual acquaintance or association based on false information can easily lead to deadly mistakes.

Speech that does not echo the party line or information that truthfully explains the nature and cause of anti-American activity can easily be construed as a threat to American policy overseas and a challenge to the current government.

3

Austrian Economics

Austrian Economics refers to free

market economies and more.

This school of thought derives from Carl Menger (1840-1921), an economist from the University of Viena. Dr. Paul says Menger made a great contribution to the theory of value. He wrote that economic value extends from the human mind alone and is not something that exists as an inherent part of goods and services. Valuation changes according to social needs and circumstances.

We need markets to reveal to us evaluations of consumers and producers in the form of a price system that works within a market setting.

Ron Paul believes that in saying this, Menger is really capturing lost wisdom that had earlier been understood by Frederic Bastiat (1801-1850), J. B. Say (1767-1832), and others.

The Austrian School champions

Private property

Free markets

Sound money

The liberal society generally

(One must remember that the word "liberal" once meant conservative. The word "liberal" is being used in that context.)

It takes into account the unpredictability of human action and the huge role of human choice in the way economics works.

John Maynard Keynes did not look at truth in developing his philosophy. He argued that savings are not a precursor to investment, but rather a drag on the economy.

He did not believe that investment, consumption, production, borrowing, and lending are integrated through the price system, homogeneous aggregates that are constantly colliding with one another.

He thought that wise central planners could know more than irrational market participants and that they could correct macroeconomic imbalances. They did this by manipulating market signals.

More often than not Keynes proposed credit expansion as the solution to all that ails us. Liberty was not an issue that concerned him. Paul said that he wrote at a time when the world fell in love with a planned economy and a planned society and lost its attachment to liberty as an ideal.

From that point on, says Paul, to this day, the Keynesian system has been in charge. However, the Austrian School has made a dramatic comeback in many different sectors, including academia. This is in a large part due to the work of large institutions such as the Mises Institute established by Ludwig Von Mises.

Mises showed that the Austrian paradigm makes more sense of the way the world works than the bundle of fallacies that characterize the Keynesian system.

Ideas, says Paul, are far more important in shaping society than bombs, armies or guns. "And this is because ideas are capable of spreading without limit. With ideas, we can make real change that lasts.

We are not cogs in a macro machine; people will always resist being treated as such. Economics should be as humanitarian as ethics, aesthetics or any field of study.

4

Bipartisanship

For more than 100 years, the dominant

**views influencing our politicians have
undermined**

*the principles of personal liberty and private
property*

The problem is these bad policies have had strong bi-partisan support. There has been no real opposition to the steady increase in the size and scope of government. "Democrats are largely and openly for government expansion. If we were to judge Republicans by their actions and not their rhetoric, we would come to pretty much the same conclusion about them."

That is the considered opinion of a veteran lawmaker, having seen it up close. Then he says something that I have believed all my life: Gridlock can be the friend of liberty.

It is better to make no law than bad law. Let the Democrats fume and fuss. When the politics of both parties are bad, there is really only one hope; that our side will keep fighting and not pen any new legislation. That's Ron Paul in a nutshell, and it's great advice.

Paul is an honest man. He believes that there is no significant difference between the two parties in:

Foreign policy

Economic intervention

The Federal Reserve

A strong executive branch and

Welfarism mixed with corporatism.

Both parties are very much alike. We have had too much bipartisanism that ignores Constitutional constraints.

The election campaigns are for one purpose only: to convince the voters that they actually have a choice. On medical care, Paul said when each party was in power they expanded it. Obama, with his new Health Care Plan; and with Republicans when Bush expanded MediCare.

The chief difference is that Republicans did not advertise it. They were ashamed of it because in doing so they broke campaign promises.

Moderates are the most dangerous in Congress; those who promise and seek bipartisanism. Compromise is too often synonymous with selling out.

Honest politicians who favor total socialized medicine are met with resistance. But moderates who get the same result through compromise slip by unnoticed.

"Compromise destroys all liberties in the name of compromise and civility," said Paul.

"Incrementalism can only be justified if we retain some of our liberties and if the size and scope of government shrinks."

Socialized medicine is a single-payer system. In the 2010 debate, the radicals who went full bore had to back off the single payer system. Yet the result was the same. We got moved significantly closer to that position.

Obama expanded unemployment benefits so that people could stay off the labor rolls; and thus they were sold a bipartisan "tax cut." It wasn't a cut at all. We just didn't have a tax increase at that time. "But moderates are, somehow, convinced that they are the saviors of the country," Paul said. They feel that they "rescued us all from the effects of philosophical differences. In fact, philosophical differences are healthy because they lead to the clarification of principles."

Ron Paul is convinced that "genuine progress is going to require more confrontation, partisanship, and serious and honest discussion of the truth about government, the economy, and every sector of American life."

What should we be looking for in a president? Paul gave the answer and I repeat it here. "It will require a politician who can hold strong to his beliefs and does not compromise his core values." He's talking about Congressmen and women as well as presidents. "How sad a state we are in when it seems like such a stretch to expect that from a politician."

5

Business Cycles

Look not at the downturn, but at the structure

of the preceding boom

Economic booms? Really? Ron Paul answers this by quoting Ludvig Von Mises in the early days of central planning. "The central bank posed a serious danger due to its ability to manipulate interest rates. Because artificially low rates cause an expansion of the money supply, these invented rates are central to understanding what causes booms."

Mises wrote in 1923 that "The first condition of any monetary reform is to halt the printing presses." Interest rates tell all businesses about the best time to expand production. When interest rates fall below their market rate, a false signal goes off that there are more saved funds for lending (from bankers) so expansion occurs.

Booms are caused by more lending. They are usually worsened by government promising bailouts to banks, and by loan guarantees, and enterprises, thereby, encouraging bad investment and business by removing the fear of failure.

Congressman Paul believes the combination of these things led to the world housing boom of the 1990s, and that same market crashed in 2008.

Previously, this affected other booms and busts: the stock market, the dot.com market, the oil market and other markets clear back to 1913, the year the Fed was founded. Business cycles before then were not so severe or as widespread because banking was not centrally controlled. Scrambling by the government and the Fed to correct things only worsened the inevitable correction.

Herbert Hoover used macro economic measures in 1930. FDR continued in that pattern. FDR and Hoover pushed the same agenda of high spending, attempted monetary expansion, controls over business and efforts to keep wages high. These are the same policies Obama is using. They led to a 20-year recession in Japan.

Both the Bush and Obama administrations, like FDR and Hoover, tried to stimulate the economy through artificial means and ended up causing tremendous damage to the economy resulting in no economic liberty.

The believers in Keynesian theory are still in charge and remain fully committed to central economic planning.

It is freedom we need, not more government interference. Our government wants more regulations. It chooses to solve our problems by even lower interest rates by creating trillions of dollars of new money while increasing spending and debt. Grade school math shows why this will not work.

6

Campaign Finance Reform

There are a lot of phony campaign

reforms on the books

It's all about curbing the buying of favors. Of course, they didn't work." All the reforms in the world won't eliminate the corruption in this system. The attempt alone threatens our ability to work within the system in order to change the system. The McCain-Feingold Act, a Bipartisan Campaign Reform Act, was the latest. In 2010 the Supreme Court ruled that McCain- Feingold restricted free speech. It is now apparent, especially following the "carnival" of big political spending during the 2012 election, that America is in drastic need of election law reform.

The size of government violates the Constitution in the enumerated powers area.

Progressives believe that government, corporations, and unions have no free speech rights, though each acts as though they do…following the flawed belief that government can regulate commercial speech in advertising.

This is especially harmful when it comes to producers of vitamins and nutritional products—companies that aren't even allowed to explain what they believe are the health benefits that come from the use of their products, thereby denying consumers useful information.

The notion that political and commercial speech are two different entities must be rejected. Speech must not be subjected to prior restraint. If the Right To Speech is lost because people belong to corporations. then radio, TV stations, newspapers, and magazines, and the Internet would be subject to prior restraint by the government.

Those who argue against permitting corporations from spending money on elections would never argue that corporate media entities such as CNN should be legally barred from influencing public opinion.

The $2,400 company donation limit per person in federal elections makes no sense. The hypocrisy of campaign giving is ridiculous. Why disallow people, associations, unions, companies and corporations from giving unlimited amounts when you allow political action groups that same advantage. Let's stop kidding ourselves. They are one and the same entities.

Government is a growth industry, and tragically so. The real obscenity is the size of government and its intrusion into every aspect of our economic and personal lives.

Campaign finance laws are not the answers. The money will just go underground or under the table. Corruption is not eliminated. It merely takes other forms.

A worse solution is taxpayer-financed elections.

7

Capital Punishment

Ron Paul is a very assertive, adroit writer

The weakest chapter of *Liberty Defined* is far better than those on capital punishment in other political books. It tells the reader that since coming to Washington D.C. he became opposed to the death penalty.

More rich than poor people are able to defeat death convictions in capital punishment trials. It is for obvious reasons—better attorneys. Paul mentions the O.J. Simpson case. "Rich people, when guilty, are rarely found guilty and sentenced to death."

Since more poor people than rich people can't afford good representation, he calls for elimination of the death penalty to make things fairer.

Dr. Paul wants "life" sentences rather than "death" sentences because later evidence has exonerated defendants on death row.

"If government can legally kill, it can do just about anything short of that," he said. "I no longer believe that government should be trusted with this power."

Our Founders left the death penalty to individual states. They wrote only three federal crimes into the Constitution: counterfeiting, treason, and piracy.

Slavery and involuntary servitude were added by the Thirteenth Amendment. The death penalty was authorized in the Coinage Act of 1792 for counterfeiting currency.

Ron Paul believes that criticism of Julian Assange, founder of Wickileaks, is unfounded: "In the end, Assange was just one man with a laptop, and he was merely releasing what is true—information that embarrassed many but harmed no one."

Dr. Paul calls it a terrible hypocrisy: "Just think of what it would be like if all those individuals in Washington responsible for counterfeiting our currency, or forcing unconstitutional penalties on us through the tax system were to be punished with death penalties."

A society dedicated to peace, human life and prosperity would more likely be achieved if we protected unborn life, opposed abortion, and rejected the death penalty.

8

Central Intelligence Agency

Orson Wells: "Whether it's a sad ending or

a happy ending depends on when the story ends."

The CIA does not serve our national security interests. "Today, if anyone criticizes the CIA or the principle of its existence, he is portrayed as being sympathetic to the terrorists."

Ron Paul believes that for the most part, the CIA has had a failed record. Its credibility dropped after participation in the lies of George W. Bush about weapons of mass destruction (WMDs) in Iraq.

Some CIA agents resigned in disgust after we found Saddam Hussein did not have WMDs, except for the gas he used to wipe out thousands of his own people including the Kurds.

Mr. Paul believes that the CIA has been totally out of control at times with its clandestine operations.

"After all," he said, "the CIA is always run by members of the administration friendly to the president who appoints them. For this reason you can't believe much of the propaganda they produce."

Congressman Paul said the Central Intelligence Agency, formed in 1947 by the National Security Act, "widely exaggerates every foreign threat to the United States. Today, the intelligence operation is huge, complex, and out of control."

The first known major use of the CIA to interfere in the election process of a country was in 1953. It involved the overthrow of the "duly elected" leader of Iran, Mohammad Mosadeck. To anyone hearing about this for the first time, it might appear grotesque and insane to even suggest that America could condone such a thing. But it *is* true and it occurs more than you think.

It is common knowledge in certain quarters—especially in Washington and among members of Congress and the administration—that the "Land of the Free" has been involved in assassinations, assisting in coups, rigging elections, and holding mock elections.

Overthrowing foreign nations is unlawful internationally, but Paul says it is legal under U.S. law including the Constitution. Congressman Paul believes it is immoral. "The CIA's involvement abroad is unbelievably complex and perverse. It is not fully monitored by Congress. Even the president doesn't have full knowledge of what the CIA does.

"The CIA is an active participant in waging wars with control of the Drone bombing of any country seen as an enemy in the future. "Obviously, this is a dangerous power to wield, especially in secret."

Rigging elections and killing our supposed enemies is now seen as a relatively acceptable policy. Through connections to international drug lords, the CIA has the power to self-finance. This isn't esoteric or private knowledge. It is known, of course, by the Director of the National Intelligence Agency (DNIA), who today is James R. Clapper, and his staff.

The CIA's clandestine activities also fund sister intelligence agencies such as the FBI and 16 sister intelligence agencies. Under control and guidance of the NIA, the CIA is a uniquely powerful entity.

It has only been since 9/11 that the U.S. has had a Director of National Intelligence (DNI). Congressman Paul boldly asserts that the CIA is too big. "It's size and scope makes it virtually impossible for the Director of National Intelligence to be a sufficient protection of America's interests."

Do not confuse the CIA or the NIA with the National Security Agency (NSA), which is an arm of the Defense Department. The NSA has been involved in cryptologic duties in analyzing foreign communications and foreign signals intelligence. It also protects U.S. government communication information systems that involve cryptography (a lot of long words) and cryptanalysis.

NSA is directed by at least a vice admiral or a lieutenant general. The director of the National Security Agency serves as the commander of the U.S. Cyber Command, currently James Clapper, and chief of the Central Security Service. By law, NSA's intelligence gathering is limited to foreign communications, but domestic incidents such as the NSA warrantless surveillance controversy did occur.

It is important not to confuse the NSA with activities of the CIA. For example, it was the NSA—not the CIA—that has done surveillance work on our own citizens. NSA's eavesdropping mission includes radio broadcasting, the Internet, telephone calls, and other intercepted forms of communication. Its secure communications mission includes military, diplomatic, and other sensitive, confidential or secret government communications.

The *Washington Post* reports that collection systems of the NSA intercept and store 1.7 billion e-mails, phone calls and other types of communications. The NSA is located at Fort Meade, Maryland (where this writer was schooled in Fort Meade's Military Intelligence School during the 1960s in aerial photo reconnaissance and other intelligence gathering techniques). NSA sorts a fraction of the above phone calls and emails into 70 separate databases."

America's spy agencies cost our taxpayers an estimated $80 billion a year. There are countries that spend far less, even per capita, than the U.S. Congressman Paul said Puerto Rico spends nothing.

Ron Paul said the CIA has been used to produce false intelligence, for example to satisfy politicians who wanted to justify America getting involved in the Iraq War. Paul, like millions of Americans, believes the war was a "disgrace" to America. The CIA is not serving our security interests by participating in overblown danger propaganda.

Thanks to the CIA, today our enemies abroad include North Korea, Yeman, and Iran. Paul said that Congress generally does not cut back CIA expenditures even when it detects corruption and waste in the agency.

Considering the CIA's involvement in drugs, is it any wonder that America finds it difficult to erect a fence encompassing our entire Mexican border? Is it also any wonder that the strongest nation on earth does not strike hard at organized drug crime that has crossed our borders and has now infiltrated many towns and cities of America, endangering our people—especially the youth of America? That is what we should call a national disgrace and a tragedy. We should quiz those kinds of presidents and Congressmen and women. If we are not satisfied with their answers we should cast them out of office in the coming 2012 elections.

9

Civil Disobedience

Like Henry David Thoreau...

Congressman Ron Paul believes in the principle of civil disobedience. When you think about it, so will you. He listed events of unrest inciting civil disobedience:

War, clear back to the Civil War

Slavery protests

Protests against the unconstitutional tax code

Martin Luther King's marches for civil rights

Ron Paul notes that protests like these are becoming more frequent. He believes that much good has come from them. Sadly, many have been imprisoned for years and sometimes for life due to protesting and the events surrounding the protests.

He admires people who protest for the greater good. But Paul stresses that his method of getting change has been through education and political action.

Congressman Paul observes that the greatest benefit in civil disobedience is the publicity it generates. On the other hand, just because a protestor is right doesn't mean change will occur. That is, he says, the courts are just as corrupt as the executive and legislative branches of government.

Paul cites examples of great changes from civil disobedience:

Martin Luther King shed light on America's segregation

King also spoke out brilliantly against the unconstitutional and pointless slaughter that occurred during the Viet Nam War.

Gandhi fought for civil liberties in India

However, King's economic views were not supported by the free market, Ron Paul observes: "Even as he (King) became more radical and correct on the Viet Nam War, he moved to the left on economic issues."

"It is not unusual for those right on war to be on the left economically or vice versa" Ron Paul said.

"Many who advocate for big government at home, advocate for a military buildup. To be consistent, one should have the same philosophy—of peace and freedom and fearing socialism and war."

The Draft

Ron Paul said that there were many unsung heroes who stood up against the involuntary servitude of the draft. He calls Heavyweight Boxing Champion Muhammad Ali one of the great examples of persecution for his beliefs. Though he had converted to the Islamic faith and was a conscientious objector, Ali was still arrested for refusing to serve in Viet Nam in 1966.

Ali said "I ain't got no quarrel with the Viet Cong."

Ron Paul stood firmly on Ali's side when he faced off against the government and was sentenced to seven years in prison. The great boxing champion didn't serve time because the Supreme Court reversed the sentence.

"That may have been the best fight he ever fought," said Paul. "But most Americans considered Ali a draft dodger."

The opposite approach to civil protests is violence. Paul warns that violence is a terrible agent of social change.

America accepts spying by the government against the enemy, but what about spying on U.S. citizens in America? Government spying on any private citizen or group is dangerous to our Fourth Amendment Rights. It was this abuse of the law that led to the tragedy at Ruby Ridge (where in 1992 government killed a woman in a pointless hunt for the husband), said Paul. They also hunted and entrapped various militia groups. Abuse of our law has been used in drug interrogation and in sting operations.

Paul believes that many are calling now for a more just system that doesn't reward the financially well connected with bailouts, "nor punish those who ask only to be totally self-reliant and not to be forced into becoming a ward or a victim of the state."

10

Conscription

America rejects slavery. It is immoral.

Ron Paul is also against forcing people

to serve in the military to wage war

Did you know that conscription was not used in the Revolutionary War?

The Constitution does not give government power to draft men into military service. Congress soundly rejected the draft during the midpoint of the British attack on the nation's capitol city of Washington in the War of 1812.

Lincoln tried to invoke a draft in the Civil War. It caused riots and offered no benefits. Woodrow Wilson was the president who caused the draft to become law in the U.S. Ron Paul said that Wilson's entry into World War I was his holy war to promote worldwide democracy, where he established the principle of the draft as a patriotic duty.

"The Fourteenth Amendment outlawing involuntary servitude," Paul said, "has been a narrowly construed amendment, not applying to the age group eighteen-to-thirty-five-year-olds which is most susceptible to military slavery."

Ron Paul recalls the draft and the income tax outrages "that should never be tolerated in a free society." He further said, "If we are to retain our liberty, one change that should be made is to repeal draft registration."

The congressman calls for a foreign policy of nonintervention, thus obviating the need for a draft.

He calls "Chicken Hawks" those who flee the draft either physically as did Bill Clinton by escaping to Canada, or by deferment as Dick Cheney did. He calls Cheney's five deferments disgraceful behavior.

When they were influencing foreign policy, the Chicken Hawks dodged the draft but later became "champions of senseless and undeclared wars."

Dr. Paul opines that in Congress there is currently no interest in reinstating the draft. "But neither is there any interest in my legislation to repeal the Selective Service Act." Ironically, the Black Caucus is the strongest current support for the draft. As America attempted to implement the draft in the 1960s, minorities were discriminated against.

Hanging in Ron Paul's office are the words of "Mr. Republican," Robert Taft.

He said: *A compulsory draft is...far more typical of a totalitarian nation than a democratic nation. The theory behind it leads directly to totalitarianism. It is absolutely opposed to the principle of individual liberty which has always been a part of American democracy (August 14, 1940).*

11

Demagogues

Politics breeds demagogues and media pundits

Ron Paul passionately dislikes demagogues because they browbeat or "play rhetorical games."

Demagoguery is the enemy of liberty. Government attracts those using power over others who enjoy using power over others, and convinces the average person that they need politicians to take care of them.

Demagogues manipulate with emotion and prejudice. The goal of demagogues is to achieve power at all costs. Dictators accomplish this by brute force. Others do it with idealistic declarations of being humanitarian saviors. All demagogues must prove that the violence is required to do good for the people.

Paul lumps all demagogues together:

1. Soviet Communists

2. French Jacobites

3. Environmental alarmists

4. Current neoconservatives

5. Cradle-to-grave welfarists

Demagogues share a belief in state power. Their technique is to take a principled stand by proponents of liberty and reason and turn it into support for something ugly and mean by gross distortion of the truth.

Who are the Demagogues? They have arguments against:

Opposing foreign aid;

Constitutional amendment to ban flag burning;

Opposition to the war on drugs;

Opposition to government that imposes cultural or religious agendas

Private property;

Defending states rights and the Tenth Amendment;

Demagogues believe property can only be used by permission of the state. They say strict private property control by individuals owning property is the most evil position anyone can take.

To exercise freedom of choice to include or exclude others is now seen as evidence of malice. The right to use property discriminately is at the core of the libertarian position. Paul believes "it is the essence of freedom of association." But freedom of association also means freedom not to associate.

All religious beliefs, political beliefs, and speech are protected, as long as it is non-violent. If government has the right to control business establishments, they have justified the intrusion of government in every aspect of our lives. The principle of private ownership is of no interest to the demagogue—even if the goals of all people of all persuasions are undermined.

"What is it that deters demagogues?" Paul asks. It is national intercourse. Those who question the drug war, the war on porn, and the Civil Rights Act of 1964, or any war, are regarded [by demagogues] as evil opponents of civilization and law and order. Honest discussions are kept at bay by the demagogue.

Dr. Paul ends this segment with an eye-catching, bold statement of truth: *"The influence that the religious, intellectual, and political demagogues have in a free society poses a greater danger to mankind than the risk of allowing a businessman to use his property as he chooses.*

12

Democracy

No system of government is good

once government has grown too large

The form of government doesn't matter too much if the government is small and non-intrusive.

The trouble with democracy is the dynamic it sets in place that changes small government into a big one. It was for that reason the U.S. Founders borrowed from the Romans the concept of a republic.

Here is what breaks down in a democracy and this is how we can correct it: People should not be empowered to take away the rights of others. But today the slogan of democracy does not mean that people prevail over government, but government prevails over the public. They do it by claiming the blessings of mass opinion. This form of government has no limits. Tyranny is not ruled out. If the demagogue is an elected official, our only recourse is to oust him/her in an election. This is another argument for Congressional term limits.

When we try to export democracy, we fail. The occupation of Iraq and Afghanistan are two good examples. It has only resulted in huge sacrifices in loss of life and wealth to the United States. National security reasons are always the excuses for invasions of other countries. Woodrow Wilson was wrong when he said that war was necessary to make the world safe for democracy.

Never allow the people to forget that America's form of government is not a pure democracy. It is a democratic republic. Pure democracy is the enemy of civil rights and always victimizes the minority. This is another reason why the Seventeenth Amendment—popular voting of senators instead of state legislatures determining the senators from each state—must be repealed. It is a bane to our free society's balance of power. Why did the thugs in Washington decide to propose the Seventeenth Amendment which ultimately replaced Article One, Section 3 of the Constitution?

Here's the proffered reason, then I'll reveal the real reason we need to change back to the practice of legislators in each state directly electing their two U.S. senators. While it is true that state legislatures were conflicted, that's no reason to toss out a true and valued balance of power provision in the Constitution.

True, controversies arose in electing senators. Delaware was without a senator for four years because of deadlocked voting. Even that doesn't mean you throw out part of the Constitution because people can't agree in particular states.

Here is why we should trash the Seventeenth Amendment:

That part of the Constitution that we had before needs to be restored to protect minority rights, to eliminate bribes, to bring the government back into balance.

If senators are popularly elected as with House members, minorities lose their ability to be a counter balance against majority rule in states and in the country as well.

The Center For Responsive Politics reported in April 2010 that there were 11,140 (I've also seen the figure of 34,000) registered lobbyists in Washington to contact and persuade a hundred senators and 435 House members. That is almost twenty-one for each representative and senator. A mite excessive, wouldn't you say?

Lobbyists work for unions, big businesses, trade and professional associations, and other groups. Many are more powerful than Congressmen themselves, earning hundreds of thousands of dollars each per year for their adroitness in getting their way with our lawmakers.

Reuters estimated that they spend upwards of a billion dollars a year jamming personal interest programs down our throats, many of which use billions of dollars of taxpayer money. Obviously they have far more power with finely dressed, housed, and wined and dined U.S. congressmen than do state legislators and citizens at large, and that is grossly wrong.

Many of these employees of corporations, unions, and professional organizations probably see U.S. senators several times a week, but how often do you think a U.S. senator meets with state representatives or with a private citizen from one of the counties of the state he represents? Almost never, except perhaps some of them once a year in local town hall meetings.

That is a tragedy and needs correcting. Senate elections are too expensive. Eliminate the

Seventeenth Amendment and you virtually eliminate costly Senate elections and lobbies that have more influence over issues and laws than anyone in the state legislature—people directly elected by the common men and women of the state. Do you see what I mean? Eliminate the Seventeenth Amendment and you eliminate the bribe-making ability of these companies. In other words, you start to "drain the Washington Swamp." Those who oppose you on this have no desire to eliminate this kind of graft and personal interest politics.

Ron Paul has promised to lead the way to elimination of this great impediment blocking sanity in Washington politics.

Another inherent evil in our democratic republic is that a majority of Americans today believe their rights are unlimited. But they interpret rights as their rights to someone else's money through government grants, bailouts, or outright fraud. Ron Paul believes the majority of Americans today believe they have a right to free medical care, education, a house, subsidized food and many other services.

What these folks don't realize is that governments have nothing to pass out, "since they produce nothing." Paul reminds us, "Anytime government provides a benefit, it must first steal it from someone else who is producing it. Thus, violating the rights of that individual. **It is important to remember that.**

I recall a time when all Americans were aghast at learning that some dictator-led South or Central American nation was "nationalizing" or stealing an American company doing business in that nation. Now it is American progressives—people like Barak Obama, Joe Biden, Nancy Pelosi, and most of the mainstream media and all of the liberal Democrats in Congress who have forgotten that this country wasn't made great because of bloated government—that want to nationalize our pocketbooks by making claims that twenty years ago were outrageous. Claims like "free" condoms for all women, "free" housing for the poor, and "free" food for the jobless.

If someone is jobless and needs food help in the Latter-day Saint church he goes to his bishop, receives a permission authorization and visits the local Bishop's Storehouse. This is not a dole because he is expected to work at the storehouse and to really look for work, not to hold out for 99 weeks pretending to be looking for the same kind of work he had which is no longer available. The Church of Jesus Christ of Latter-day Saints program is from God. It believes a dole discourages men and women and is not God's way. The next president of the United States should work to adopt a similar program for the nation.

I know of no better way to encourage unemployment than these outrageous demands on hard working taxpayers. All of the government medical care legislation must be either revamped downward or totally eliminated to stem this national trend. As a basic Constitutional right, man was endowed with the right to ownership of property. That means what is mine is mine, not yours. Have it any other way and you have Arab style riots in the streets, burning of private property and killing of innocent people. It all stems from folks not being well grounded in human rights and these rights aren't limited to "life, liberty, and the pursuit of happiness." They include the word "property."

In fact, our founders were going to use that term instead of "happiness" but because black slaves were considered "property" they substituted happiness for property. But the historical and legal meaning is clear.

A majority vote should never be used to justify the undermining of human rights. Democracy is not the same as freedom and prosperity. Medical care is not a right. Government should not provide Medical care. It is just one of many ways our government has grown too big and needs whittling down.

13

Discrimination

As defined by Webster, there is

nothing wrong with discrimination

Discrimination merely seems to choose this over that. It is also known as having a discriminatory taste or of making fine distinctions—both of which are pluses. We discriminate as to whom we invite to our homes; whom we talk to and whom we marry. It is a right we cherish. But Congressman Paul believes banning discrimination in some government programs makes sense.

Getting ahead because of special privileges granted by government violates principles of individual rights and private property ownership. So does falling behind because of arbitrary penalties.

Free societies allow people to be creeps and associate with crooks if they want to. We can pick and choose our associates. Social and economic disapproval works better than government regulation. For example, forced hiring practices have no place in a free society. But the voluntary association approach does not have to achieve integration in the churches by anyone's standards.

Paul believes that almost all churchgoers attend segregated congregations by pure choice. Even after decades of school integration by federal mandates, the vast majority of black and white children are still in segregated schools. Separation seems to be the choice. The congressman believes that seeking equal justice before the law—not forced integration—should be the goal.

Let's not increase hostility and class warfare between groups. Falsely and loudly accusing someone of racism or antisemitism if the person is not in agreement with reparations is the worst kind of bigotry.

"Such hypocrisy has destroyed a lot of people's reputations and lives," says Paul. "It does great harm to any effort to bring people together voluntarily. " For example, the mere offer of financial giveaways to hurricane victims invites every manner of public corruption. It also creates a moral hazard.

Moral hazards in insurance parlance are those risks brought about by crooked actions of insured parties designed to get non-covered losses paid or to profit more greatly than the policy anticipated by virtue of increasing the risk and thus increasing resulting losses.

An example of this is when a poorly maintained furnace explodes, causing fire and other damage to the entire home and personal property. In other words, it's a loss waiting to happen. Risk inspectors, adjusters, and underwriters do their best to avoid insuring moral hazards; investigations strive to reveal or catch the problems, thus allowing the carrier to either deny payment, cancel policies, or refuse to renew a policy. Policies are underwritten based on certain standards of care expected from policyholders. These kinds of losses mitigate against the rates of other insureds, tending to drive them up.

If there are many of these kinds of insureds in a particular locale, carriers make strategic underwriting decisions to either change the policies or leave that area as Farmers, Allstate, and State Farm did in South Florida following Hurricane Andrew. The policies were written to exclude the poor quality of construction typical in low cost, older housing.

High winds flattened houses that were not in condition required by local building codes. To be specific, these homes lacked metal roof straps every sixteen inches that would have held the roofs in place, diminishing the chance of a lot of damage. Another defect was that these homes were built too low in the ground, being susceptible to surface water and flood water which is never covered in homeowner policies without specific flood insurance riders.

One problem: Insurance Commissioner, Bill Nelson, made an executive decision requiring payment of those claims in Homestead, Florida where no coverage existed. This liberal attitude provided the impetus for Democrat Bill Nelson to run for the U.S. Senate where he currently serves. He was so much "help" to the people in Homestead that he was sure he could be of similar "help" to all of Florida.

The carriers were allowed to stop renewing business or writing new homeowner business—thus leaving the state. But Nelson required that they deposit large sums of money for reserves for new carriers to begin operation under close scrutiny of the state insurance department.

Were the carriers discriminated against. Of course, but in Nelson's mind it was for the greater good. This is a phrase progressives like to attach to any contract they want to break by government power.

Is this reverse discrimination? Yes, because in the end, those losses were spread around to other insureds and their premiums were raised because of this event and due to no cause of their own.

In the federal government, fraud and manipulation also occurs when FEMA orders a person living in a flood plain to rebuild his home outside the boundaries of the flood plain; but often government agencies look the other way, paying for the damage the second time anyway at the same location, increasing the chance for future moral-hazard losses.

Governments make poor payers of property damage because of the fraud they overlook and political pressures they respond to. They often exhibit indifference to the truth, and the favoritism and discrimination they create by their actions is obvious, not to mention the greater burdens they place on all other taxpayers living on high ground and complying with building codes.

The government doesn't produce anything. It has no money, except that which it takes from individuals in the form of taxes or creates out of thin air by floating a treasury bond they hope China or some other entity will buy.

14

Education

There is no constitutional authority for

the federal government to be involved in education,

regardless of what the Supreme Court has said

Likewise, there is no constitutional provision for states and communities to be involved in education. Until the twentieth century, education was the responsibility of the church, the family, and the local community.

Only in the past sixty years has the federal government taken over education. It did so by raising national taxes and returning part of those taxes to states to finance and direct education at all levels under the guise of equalizing educational opportunity for all Americans.

Whenever taxes go to Washington and make an end run back to the states in the form of services, the overhead eats up fifty-percent or more of the tax dollar.

That overhead resides in big government bureaucracies, in their buildings, in employee salaries and benefits—and government employees are glutinous. Federal public employee salaries and retirement pay are usually more than twice that paid in the private sector. Which argues the point that Federal Government is not the most efficient way to run things.

Gradually, the Feds—the liberals in Washington—maneuvered and schemed, finally creating a national education department, setting and dictating a national education policy—once sovereign territory of local communities and citizens—one that could be manipulated and changed every year if they wanted according to the politics, whims, political persuasion, and personal principles of a few at the top.

Thus, government grows like a weed and gets farther away from the people, explaining it away in terms of equal opportunity for all. This is a progressive's poor excuse for taking greater power from the people and making national government larger and all-powerful.

There is no evidence that the quality of education has improved. In science and math American students place next to the lowest in the world—even against those nations that spend less than half that spent by American schools on education. Then you ask, "Does America have an education problem? Could it be that a program like this administered by Washington cannot succeed when you place the power so far away from the people? As president, Ron Paul abolishes the national department of education and allows states to keep enough money to administer their own program.

There is evidence that more people go to college and the cost of higher education has skyrocketed. There is more centralized control at grade school and high school levels. This is where parents have less control over their schools today. In addition says Ron Paul, "There has definitely been more violence, more drugs, and more dropouts associated with more centralized control."

The regulations are extremely tight on alternative schools. Paul laments that this keeps the market from operating as it should.

What are the alternatives or helps to avoid public schooling?

Private schools

Home schooling

Vouchers

Tax credits

Charter schools

Too often these efforts do not eliminate the power of the state to control the curriculum. Congressman Paul believes that tax credits are best; vouchers, however, invite bureaucratic control of their usage and are unfairly distributed.

Not long ago, the Republican Party Platform argued for getting rid of the Department of Education, inserting the disastrous No Child Left Behind program. Now, national control of all schools is firmly a bipartisan effort.

Ron Paul reports that court rulings on discipline, decorum, and correctness have intimidated many dedicated teachers and curtailed any creativity they might have had.

Classics and foreign languages were taught to the Founders in home schools. Not so today, perhaps until the student reaches high school level.

The current system has driven many state school systems into bankruptcy. Dr. Paul blames extravagance in building ornate physical structures, while neglecting quality education. This has added greatly to the debt burden of local and state budgets.

The National Education Association (NEA) is really just a teacher union. The NEA is responsible for structural expenses and the huge teacher salaries and health and retirement benefits that dwarf those paid in private enterprise. The future responsibility to pay for teacher salaries and benefits will require constant and careful review.

Many state pension funds are not solvent. Whether retired teachers and other public employees will receive their benefits is questionable.

Ron Paul then brings up the value of the dollar these people—actually, all of us— will receive. He said he is certain that the federal government will bail the teachers out, but at what dollar value? Then what about the rest of us?

Paul sees no effort to reform the vastly inefficient and ineffective schools. "In reality," he laments, "the whole system may self-destruct by poor performance and runaway costs."

We have been told that our free public education system made America what it is today. "Soon they will be forced to quit making that claim," said the Congressman. "Someday, eliminating federal controls may be achievable."

This far-sighted leader claims that local control of schools is one of the answers. Ron Paul would make local school boards the owners of the schools. They would set curriculum, discipline standards, and taxes. "This system isn't perfect, but it is vastly better than a Washington-run system with an economic czar using the education system for propaganda, perpetuating the falsehoods of the state and the so-called benefits of a powerful central government.

"Thank goodness for the Internet, Amazon, and the thirst for truth," he said, "and that no government is too big to silence."

15

Empire

Congressman Ron Paul tells why many

across the globe hate us for

being a terrible empire

The world hates America for:

1. Invading their country

2. Supporting dictatorships

3. Starving people through sanctions

4. An unprecedented military empire of global reach

5. The U.S. being an empire by any definition, and quite possibly the most aggressive, extended, and expansionist in the history of the world.

Finally, Paul says, "Would we, as American citizens, like it if some superpower were doing this to us?"

Due to geopolitical events moving much faster today than the Roman Empire, America's empire will be much shorter—230 years compared to 450 years.

Why? Chalk it up to modern technology—weapons of speed of travel and communications. Paul agonizes over the fact that today's military and CIA efforts are almost totally unrestrained by the U.S. Congress.

America's empire has orchestrated military coups against governments we find dispensable. Why and which ones? Iran-contra-type financing is a tool used to circumvent any effort by Congress to restrain clandestine activity that promotes our empire. We have set up many South American dictators, but here are just a few examples of corrupt dictators in other countries we set up and later toppled after they had served our purpose:

Egypt—Mubarak

Indonesia—Suharto

Middle East—Osama bin Laden

Pakistan—Ayub Khan and Yahya Khan

Iran—the Shah

Libya—Muammar Qaddafi

Iraq—Saddam Hussein

Pakistan—Pervez Musharraf

We gave them the same weapons and technology that are killing our soldiers today. The practice of nation building and democratizing other countries is a sad 'quick fix' for whatever policy the US seeks. One doesn't have to be an expert in foreign policy to see that it no longer works. Look at Sudan. We have allowed atrocities, as bad as or worse than Saddam Hussein and the Shah, to kill and displace millions of human beings.

It's a puppet show and the puppeteers are following a script. Even our own experts say the world is onto us and won't take it anymore. The US arms the same elements that they expect to fight in the future … they allow a crisis to evolve in order to market intervention to the American public and select allies. Ron Paul has the answer: bring all of our troops home and quickly end the empire with all it's games.

Eighty billion dollars are spent on U.S. intelligence gathering yearly—and what do we have to show for it? This money has virtually no oversight by the U.S. Congress. When things go bad—often due to our intelligence efforts—it results in the use of our military at great cost to taxpayers. Congress always agrees "for national security reasons." These efforts have led to a worldwide presence of U.S. troops, turmoil and war after war, with hundreds of millions of people killed or left homeless.

America has been brainwashed into thinking national security demands an international U.S. presence. Our worldwide military invites the distribution of our way of life, just as it did to the Roman Empire.

Congressman Paul asks if we have crossed the point of no return in world military buildup. Have we crossed our own Rubicon? He maintains that America has crossed the line—America is a world empire. We assumed the role long ago of worldwide military arbiter or administrator of military power so that our domination continues to expand and grow.

America has more military might than all the rest of the world combined. The danger to America lies from within, especially in our lost liberties. Is our republican form of government salvageable? After asking this thought-provoking question,

Ron Paul goes on for twenty pages, then asks:

How long can the dollar reign?

Will our system have a sudden demise? He does not believe our empire can or should go on and on in its present form. But, rather, like the Soviet Union, the Congressman says it will come to a sudden end when other nations will no longer let us borrow and our promise is worthless.

What can save us? Ron Paul believes "we must confront this growing empire. We have no place on earth to run. We must defend our American way of life with the rightness of liberty and what our Founders created for us; we cannot acquiesce. We must fight in a loyal, peaceful way."

Ron Paul quotes a favorite of many, Victor Hugo:

There is nothing more powerful than an idea whose time has come."

The American Empire should not be one of them. Dr. Paul said that we are in an ideological struggle. He sincerely believes it is one we can win. "But it cannot be won without addressing the status of the American empire." Perpetual war and preparation for war is incompatible with a free society. There are those in America who say they oppose big government. Yet they can't bring themselves around to criticize one of the biggest arms of government, militarism and war, including so-called preventive war.

"War feeds on the growth of the state." **Conversely, "the state is nourished on the liberties of the people."** It's simple: bigger government means fewer liberties.

The choice is liberty or dictatorship (authoritarianism), and republic or empire. Paul draws a clear line in the sand: "The notion that we can cut government and nourish and maintain empire is preposterous." Yet that is exactly what other candidates advocate.

Preventive War

The Congressman loudly proclaims that "a country that supports preventive war and allows assassination of its own citizens and endless torture can hardly be called a republic."

Our empire—with troops situated throughout the world—is every bit as pervasive as the British Empire at its zenith. Unfortunately, those who oppose preventive war and occupation are criticized for being unpatriotic.

"Our foreign policy of interventionism has brought the worst out in those who support the empire," said Ron Paul. He asserts that empires redefine patriotism just as welfare redefines charity. The two go together. The two ideas mean that the state should be master.

None of this has Mr. Paul's approval or concurrence:

Unfortunately today, death and injury are seen as small prices to pay for the so-called benefits of empire. Our young warriors have been taught to believe that their bravery in battle in foreign wars is a small price to pay for freedom at home. Is that really what the Iraq and Afghanistan wars were about, freedom at home? In some measure it was because defense experts tell us that we and our allies have all but destroyed al Qaeda in Afghanistan to the point that it does not present a present danger here at home.

Unfortunately, much of this is propaganda fed to American citizens. Alleged military experts and especially generals and elected officials are sure the al Qaeda and foreign operatives and terrorists would be fighting on our shores today had we not invaded Iraq and Afghanistan. This is sheer nonsense, though it has been the official party line of the Democratic and Republican Parties and both George W. Bush and Barak Obama and their administrations. It's almost as if there's an unseen power guiding this.

Both the writer of this book and Congressman Paul believe this has been terribly overblown. It is propaganda to conform with someone's desire to fight foreign wars, even when there is no clear and present danger cited above. It conforms exactly to the current military-industrial complex view of military expansionism, which Mr. Paul has been quite explicit about—that this "empire view of things" must end at the peril of losing our liberties. You can't have the empire and our liberties. What you get is dictatorship and that is the direction in which America is headed as Obama's actions each day indicate.

Did the fact that by all historical accounts the United States lost the Viet Nam War and had to withdraw under extreme pressure from the Viet Cong mean that America thereafter was any less safe at home from foreign invasion? No, it didn't. These wars are all fought for bogus reasons that have very little to do with America's national security interests at home.

Millions of American troops have been killed or wounded over ill-conceived aggressive wars abroad. We have been fighting meaningless foreign wars for more than seventy years. During that time, politicians and Pentagon leaders have hatched this empire building principle. Their propaganda says that that fighting wars abroad makes America safer at home. In truth, it rarely does.

Why America Is Hated Abroad

There is a great deal of truth to the assertion that these wars cause foreign animosity toward America, rather than creating good public relations. As Paul asserts, many believe that had we not fought in Arab states we probably would not have had 9/11. Nor would we be in our current mess internationally, with hatred of Americans in most of the Arab states and dwindling resources to play this dangerous game. We're broke!

How would you like it, Mr. Paul asks, if someone invaded and occupied us? How would you feel toward that country and its soldiers that robbed us of our freedoms, killed innocent family members and friends and neighbors? We would forever be at odds with them, just as the Finnish people are still very suspicious of Russia for invading them and robbing them of a sizeable piece of their land after the Winter War of 1939. I have lived there and I can tell you of the hatred the Fins have for the Russians, as opposed to the appreciation and love they have for the west.

Dr. Paul says, "Unfortunately today, death and injury are seen as small prices to pay for the so-called benefits of empire."

"Why do many people on the left fail to see any connection between a policy of perpetual war and the loss of civil liberties at home? Many do not believe their party's rhetoric. This deception only facilitates big government and its deficits, and the diminishing of individual liberties that they say they are fighting to save."

Paul is so right on this. He says "Tea Party activists will often claim to oppose the system of tax and spend, bailouts, and socialism. But to the extent that they uncritically defend U.S. foreign policy, they are supporting all the policies they are claiming to be against."

***Author's Note: In the above statement, "Tea Party activists" include all of the original nine Republican presidential candidates except one, Ron Paul.

Until and unless other republicans lead out as Mr. Paul has done on this vital issue, the American public should stand true to their colors and flatly reject every one of those other candidates. They are not true conservatives and without Ron Paul's presence in the White House there will be no leadership and progress on this important issue. The "Washington swamp" cannot be drained because while candidates talk the talk, they are unable or unwilling to walk the walk.

Paul said America's republic is in trouble: "America is on its last legs and the military approach is impractical and unsustainable for the twenty-first century."

America is now faced with fourth generation warfare—gorilla resistance. The two primary forces have been the Taliban and al Qaeda. A lot more men and women than died in 9/11 have been sacrificed in the ten years following 9/11. There still is no peace and stability in Iraq and Afghanistan, despite the fact that Osama bin Laden was captured and killed.

By any measure, now that Egypt and Libya are "liberated," the Taliban and al Qaeda and the Muslim Brotherhood are winning the wars.

Paul has this to say about Israel: "The more America defends Israel, that will only drive Iran and Iraq closer to China, our enemy. "No one running for president, except Ron Paul, has dared to make this tough, insightful statement.

The Congressman believes that these wars are propagandized with false statistics that are intended to justify the four trillion dollars America has spent in useless wars over the last ten years. "In truth, many of our kills are freedom fighters defending their homeland. If the American voters knew this they would be upset."

"The longer these wars go on, the greater is the danger to our national security and our financial well being." Terrorism is a criminal act, not an act of war. But to eradicate terrorists some people have been known to advocate extreme measures—even nuclear warfare, and they care little about the liberty we lose because of the fear of terrorism.

The Departments of Defense and Veteran Affairs employ almost a third of all of the 2.7 million federal employees or about 817,000 people across the globe. In third place is the Department of Homeland Security with 129,000 employees. These figures are remarkable and are that large primarily because of the fear of terrorism strikes the hearts of U.S. citizens. The war on terrorism is connected to our military efforts in the Middle East and to our homeland defense buildup.

But the war on terrorism is no more a true war than the war on poverty, illiteracy, or drugs. Paul paraphrased another congressman who said, "It's all necessary because people are too stupid to take care of themselves."

Neoconservatives

Dr. Paul said neo-cons embrace lies. "Stretching the truth and lying are permissible under the code of The Noble Lie used to secure partisan support."

He says some congressmen moan a little, but funds are always made available "for fear of being called un-American or a member of the 'blame America' crowd, and being characterized as being weak on national defense." Congressman Paul remembers having other congressmen blaming what they termed a hate-filled Islam religion as the source of our problems and we must pursue the war on terrorism at all costs, even if it does mean preventive war.

Sadly, many Americans cannot believe that America's own policies contribute to suicide tension. Such an attitude is treason. "Demagogy, lying, or denying that no unintentional consequences or blowback result from our invasion, occupation and bombing of other nations, basically Arab and Muslim countries, presents the greatest danger to our country's security, freedom and property."

In any criminal act, police look for motives. Yet neo-cons say the sole reason is religious. Neo-cons can't believe that terrorism is sometimes caused by the blowback phenomena the CIA identified many years ago.

Paul believes that much terrorism is caused by people who want to prove a point or to draw attention to injustices. He notes that there hasn't been a major terrorism attack for ten years. He believes that this proves a fallacy. There was a lot of misplaced effort to fight terrorism in the Middle-East which has resulted in needless death and destruction.

Our policies that have us spending some hundred fifty billion dollars a year for homeland security are flawed. Congressman Ron Paul is not alone in his assessment. As political scientist John Mueller notes, in most years allergic reactions to peanuts, deer in the road, and lightening have all killed about the same number of Americans as terrorism. In 2001, their banner year, terrorists killed one twelfth as many Americans as the flu and one fifteenth the number killed by car accidents. By any statistical measure, the terrorist threat to America has always been low.

According to Ben Friedman in a World AfterNet article, all of the steps of terrorism are doable, especially for a professional terrorist organization, as Al Qaeda proved. "But conventional analysis of terrorism ignores the second reason terrorism is not so easy: today's terrorist organizations are not as capable as Al Qaeda once was, especially when it comes to operating overseas. One possible exception, Lebanon's Hezbollah, is no longer in the business of attacking the United States. Friedman says the war in Afghanistan and a worldwide policing effort against Al Qaeda shattered the main terror network that menaced the United States. "In its place are disaggregated set of extremist Sunni groups who share little more than Al Qaeda's ideology, and pockets of unaffiliated fellow travelers. This network is linked by personalities, websites, and in some cases financing, but they do not cooperate much, and lack the training and experience the core of Al Qaeda had. These groups will struggle to train operatives, get false documents, and coordinate men and material abroad."

Friedman observes major terror attacks have recently struck in countries that have large pockets of Muslims; and that there is no similar large group in America. Terrorism has occurred in London, Madrid, Jakarta, Bali, Riyadh, Sharm-el-Sheik, Istanbul, Casablanca, Manila, and especially Iraq. But while some of these attacks, including the London subway bombing, may involve men with links to foreign groups, the impetus of the attacks came from local groups, which bodes well for a nation like America..

Financial information from Homeland Security books show total liabilities of about $85 million including U.S. Customs and Border Protection, Federal Emergency Management Agency, U.S. Coast guard, U.S. Citizenship and Immigration

Services, Federal Law Enforcement Training Center, the National Protection and Programs Directorate, and U.S. Immigration and Customs Enforcement.

America's policies are flawed. Paul would like someone in the administration to step forward and admit their mistakes. That will never happen, not until we have someone like Ron Paul in the White House. He doesn't advocate blaming America over a few bad decisions made by our leaders. Obviously, these leaders were Barak Obama and George W. Bush.

Blind obedience to government-driven war propaganda has to stop. It is more likely that an American will die from being hit by lightning than from a terrorist attack. Of the 14,800 homicides in the U.S. in 2009, only fourteen were caused by terrorists. Between 35,000 and 40,000 deaths occur each year on our highways.

Cicero was assassinated for his efforts to save the rule of law. He refused to join Julius Caesar's betrayal of the Roman constitution. Caesar was assassinated after becoming dictator for life on the ides of March.

Ron Paul predicts a bloody reaction is coming by those who wield the power over the military-industrial complex if anyone challenges the

American Empire. He sees as a moral imperative the taking down of the Empire, which includes the evil part of our political process—the Washington Swamp.

What President Paul Would Do:

The liberal know-nothing media must be challenged, the monetary system changed, and the economy needs booting up by large corporate and private business tax cuts. Paul will repeal the Obama rules and regulations. He will let "capital" know they can invest in America now with renewed vigor and with the confidence to compete with the world and bring those lost jobs back to America. With this and no more foreign aid to China, he will announce a new era—America is back, America will again prevail on the economic playing field. Forget 2040, China, it isn't going to happen.

On the contrary, if Paul is not elected and we get a progressive, moderate or neo-con in the White House you can bet on four more years of market contractions, loss of jobs and a sputtering, moribund economy. "Concentration of material well being and neglect of moral principles that underpin material abundance will result in the loss of property, peace, and liberty," he says.

The American Empire is the enemy to American freedom. It is every bit as much an enemy of the American citizen as it is of its victims around the world." When will America realize this and stand up and fight?

16

Envy

Envy is the painful awareness

of another's good fortune

Envy is worse than jealousy, which is wanting what another has, because very often it is a desire to end that good fortune of another. Envy is one of the seven deadly sins.

Redistribution of Wealth

Paul believes envy is behind forces of redistribution policy in America. It is the secret motivation behind the unrelenting attacks on the rich. Envy is what people refer to as the green-eyed monster. Here are the practical emanations of envy:

Progressive income tax

Inheritance tax

All other public policies rooted in envy

The above political actions cause people to pull back from doing great things. People who might otherwise pursue wealth building—which is a good thing if it ends in job creation—pull back, influenced by forces of the law.

Congressman Paul calls it institutionalized immorality. "Our laws should elicit from us the best that we have to offer. It should appeal to the highest impulses of our nature.

This is America, right? Everyone should have the same opportunity to succeed. People come from other nations just to live out "The American Dream," which is not limited to, but includes, the chance to really do well financially if that person is willing to work hard enough to succeed. There are countless examples of people who have come to America, started up businesses, and done very well.

Dr. Paul believes America doesn't have to be number one in everything. We should not consider the Chinese or others who are better than us in some ways as enemies. "We need to learn to be inspired by the success of others."

17

Evolution Versus Creation

Congressman Ron Paul is a man of God

Dr. Paul says the recognition of an evolutionary process doesn't support atheism, nor should it diminish one's view about God and the universe. This is a debate about science and religion, and he wishes it could be more civil and not involve politicians at all. It's an academic debate only.

Both sides want to use the state to enforce their views on others. "One side," he says, "doesn't mind using force to expose others to prayer and professing their faith. The other side demands that they have the right never to be offended and demands prohibition of any public expression of faith."

America does not have a state religion, or even a movement to form one. State religion was one of the primary things people from Holland and Great

Britain fled from and the reason they came to America. They wanted basic freedom of speech, assembly, and religion. They wanted to escape heavy-handed states that taxed them on almost everything they possessed. Theocracies are still being imposed on people across the globe.

Many today believe taxes, rules, and regulations are getting out of hand even in America, and that we must elect honest officials who will fight big government, not pander to bureaucracy. Unfortunately, we find these big government advocates on both sides of the isle.

Questions of God And Evolution

Why should a presidential candidate be quizzed on whether he or she believes in evolution? Paul wonders if such questions are designed to embarrass candidates for no good reason. Thomas Jefferson said, "It does me no injury for my neighbor to say there are twenty Gods or no God. It neither picks my pocket nor breaks my leg."

However, in a school setting evolution is a major topic of discussion. School curriculum and standards of behavior are dictated by the federal government, particularly the Department of Education and federal courts.

"The Constitution does not prohibit religious expression in public places," said Paul. "But the modern interpretation demands strict prohibition of public expressions. Sadly, at the forefront of this silly position are the evangelical atheists. Today, athletes can't even have a public prayer before a game between schools. What we need is a broad-based tolerance, not more court cases enforcing our activities."

Ron Paul supports the following argument against evolution. "If it is an active principle, why is man devolving from good behavior to bad—and why are there more murders and other crimes per capita today than decades ago?"

18

Executive Power

Rarely does an elected leader truly resist

the temptation to exert power over the people

Here are Congressman Ron Paul's words: "Lust for power is a human trait. The Founders' answer to greedy lawmakers and leaders were checks and balances. The federal government was restricted to power as found in the Constitution. Article One, Section Three defines the limited power the federal government has over the people."

The fifty-six Founders would not have approved the Constitution "without a clear limitation of the powers of the federal government." Study the language and the debates. Study the Federalist Papers.

Understanding Ron Paul's Mind:

Paul claims there is not a hint of evidence that the Interstate Commerce Clause and the General Welfare Clause justified our current coercive federal welfare state. Yet, over the years, especially since FDR worked his evil magic on the Great Depression during the awful 1930s, a modern interpretation was forced on us by our courts and taught in our schools. Ron Paul adroitly observes that this means the Constitution could be changed at will by the three branches of government and without proper amendments.

That is because all they had to do was call it "interstate commerce" and it could be regulated without limit. Congressman Paul adds that even martial law could be justified "according to the demands of general welfare."

"George Bush used his power in near dictatorial ways, passing the Homeland Security Presidential Directive in 2007 that gave him near dictatorial powers in event of national emergency," said Paul.

"The Constitution is a dead letter under these circumstances," he claims. "What permits government to regulate every aspect of American labor contracts? It is a radical policy in the court case of National Relations Board v. Jones and Laughlin Steel Corporation."

It is what radically undermined the Interstate Commerce Clause, with the court justifying their ruling by saying the Tenth Amendment "is but a truism" and did not limit federal powers. That was United States v. Darby Lumber in 1941.

Ron Paul believes the separation of powers between the national government and states has "virtually disappeared." All of it was done in the past ten years. But "because everything that government touches completely fails, people are debating the Tenth Amendment again."

Shift of Power To Executive Branch

The Congressman believes an all-powerful executive branch is as big a problem as the sovereignty taken from the states. It is clear the Constitution made Congress the most important branch of government, but today it is the weakest, said Paul. Congress was supposed to have decided issues of war, money, international and domestic trade laws, spending, taxes, and foreign relations. Today, these issues are the responsibility of the president—especially without congressional input.

We know how the progressive Barak Obama feels about this—exactly the same as the progressive George W. Bush felt about it. But how many of the nine candidates running for the Republican nomination for the presidency of the United States feel the same way as Ron Paul about smaller government? Perhaps one does—fellow libertarian and former New Mexico Governor Gary Johnson of New Mexico. But only to a degree is this candidate antagonistic to presidents or governors grabbing more power.

The current front-runners, Romney and Perry, are not going to campaign for less power in the executive branch and maybe Johnson won't either. He built 500 miles of new roads in New Mexico without legislative approval. He rammed it through as an executive order because the representatives of the people opposed it. That kind of Obama-like activity takes a chunk out of freedom.

Ron Paul says Congress gave up its prerogatives without a fight. Does that mean Paul's limited-government iconoclasm is dangerous? No, it doesn't—just the contrary. More voters should side with Paul on limited government because the Constitution and the Founders saw the wisdom of limited government. Why do you think the Puritans and others thereafter came to America if it wasn't to throw off heavy burdens imposed by kings? It was to escape big, powerful government in the form of wicked monarchs and tyrants that exist even today, imposing heavy fines and regulations on private enterprise and the little guy here in America and aggrandizing themselves with the perks of power, including expensive trips for their family and supporters to exotic places, taking up half or all of lavishly-appointed hotels, always working against that wanted by representatives of the people, the House of Representatives.

Don't kid yourself! Barak Obama's excesses amounted to multi-millions of dollars. Americans paid for it during a time when almost ten percent of them were jobless and the economy was in recession. If that isn't presidential hypocrisy, I don't know what is. Obama's low job approval numbers reflect America's angst against a profligate leader.

Too many members of Congress have been taught that for America to survive, we had to have a super-strong president. It can only be achieved at the expense of the peoples' liberty. Excessive dictatorial powers in the hands of an arrogant president are the envy of the enemy of the liberties that the U.S. Constitution was supposed to protect.

Paul Gives Examples:

Our system of education

Our school systems have brainwashed the public to believe that to be truly a great leader, the president had to be a wartime president. Many presidents welcomed wars, or manufactured them, and each time liberties of the people were lost.

Presidents now decide on war and Congress acquiesces. The War Powers Resolution of 1972 was and is a failure. Instead of restraining a president, it gives a president authority to pursue war for ninety days without Congressional approval. Since World War II, all of our wars have been fought without Congressional authority.

Trade Treaties

Trade treaties are entered into prior to receiving Congressional approval. The Founders were suspicious of entangling agreements with foreign nations. The Constitution requires a two-third vote of the Senate prior to entering into a trade treaty. Today, however, our presidents do about anything they like in this area. That is why we have international trade agreements like World Trade Organization (WTO), Coalition For Fair Trade Rules (CFTR), and the North American Free Trade Agreement (NAFTA). They sacrifice national sovereignty to international government organizations.

If there is a dispute between nation parties to NAFTA, for example, the WTO arbitrates the disagreement. In theory that may sound good, but in practice it creates animosities. It is better that nations arbitrate their own disagreements.

But let there be no doubt, Congress did finally ratify NAFTA. More Republicans than Democrats voted for it, but not Ron Paul. While Ron Paul backs free trade in theory, he opposes many of the institutions and arrangements to NAFTA, for example, those that promote it in practice. Actually, Paul's position is to oppose WTO and NAFTA precisely because they are not about so-called "free trade... in practice." As Paul said on the floor during the CAFTA debate:

"If we were interested in free trade, as the pretense is, you could initiate free trade in one small paragraph. This bill is more than one thousand pages, and it is merely a pretext for free trade. At the same time we talk about free trade, we badger China, and that is not free trade. I believe in free trade, but this is not free trade. This is regulated, managed trade for the benefit of special interests (eg.:Big Pharma and Agriculture). That is why I oppose it.

Unfortunately, these agreements can supersede state laws as well. All of this is counter to our constitution. If the people wanted the president and international trade organizations to control our trade, they should have sought approval by creating a constitutional amendment, but they didn't.

Tongue in cheek, Ron Paul may have said that there was an easier way. Supersede the Constitution and write an executive order signed by the president. Who needs the Constitution?

How are these bureaucracies governed that the executive creates? The president's executives write the rules without Congressional oversight. As Paul says: "The agencies become both the policeman and judge in a monstrous system of administrative justice. Under this system the defendant is considered guilty until proven innocent." Congressman Paul believes that the average citizen lacks funds to defend himself in court when confronted with our federal government and especially with a foreign government.

Life in the private enterprise trenches, where most of us live, contrasts with rich lawmaker bureaucrats who "swell their ranks with constant pay raises and job security.

War Powers—Most Dangerous

Paul believes that the war powers assumed by the presidents during periods of conflict may be the executive branch's most dangerous assumption of power. Economic controls came during wars. Three presidents—Roosevelt, Truman, and Nixon—ordered wage and price controls.

Both Obama and Bush used what is called "state secret privileges." Now Obama can claim that privilege and refuse to release information even without a showing that these so-called secrets or evidences would threaten national security.

A president can also cite this to hold suspects indefinitely and without charges being made. Bush massively expanded executive powers this way. The Freedom of Information Act has not limited this power court approach. In addition, America has what is termed the Foreign Intelligence Surveillance Act. It, too, has increased the dangers of runaway executive power in the post 9/11 era.

Today, the executive branch can ignore a civil trial verdict of innocence if the administration still deems the person a threat; and that person can be thrown in prison indefinitely.

The current executive branch has encroached on judicial powers as well. Anyone, including an American, can be targeted for assassination, no charges filed, no trial held, no rights guaranteed. People can be arrested and held indefinitely, no charges made.

Some of us were worried that Barak Obama would override the right of habeas corpus and jail untold numbers of people. FDR jailed 110,000 Japanese-Americans during World War II and just before his third re-election. It reduced the number of voters opposing him, for one; secondly, he solidified his base by coming down hard on anyone even slightly Japanese—including entire Japanese families who were thrown in jail together. This author has written a novel about such internments on a massive scale in our day called *The Exterminator*, soon to come out in another edition called *Death By Executive Order* available as an e-book at Amazon and Barnes and Noble. Visit Don White's Landing Page for links: **http://whitewriters.blogspot.com/**

I don't know why we aren't better educated on internment. They did it in Ireland and in other war-torn countries. Lincoln did it. It's a terrible thing, but because leaders want to show to their base their disgust with a certain segment of society in order to win re-election, they resort to the terrible means. Don't be surprised that a losing Barak Obama may also resort to this tactic in his bid for re-election sometime soon, before the November 4, 2012 national elections. Obama already has that right. Habeas corpus no longer exists, according to Congressman Ron Paul. The dubious reason given is that national security would be threatened if we held those trials. Don't get upset and start worrying. Use that energy to back a real patriot, Ron Paul. Even if the congressman is not elected, his ideas will live on—possible in the person of his son, Senator Rand Paul. Change takes time. Talk to your friends about this book and his 50 principles necessary to maintain liberty in America. Liberty was never won in a day, it requires constant urging, fighting, speaking out, and utmost vigilance to protect our sacred rights.

On battlefields, military courts can be justified; but any president, without legislative authority, can claim emergency and hold secret trials, moving American to a totalitarian state.

Presidents now exert huge power with appropriated funds. President Bush took millions of dollars earmarked for Afghanistan and started the war with Iraq.

Presidents can borrow money from the Federal Reserve. The Fed can also loan or give money to other banks or to foreign governments without congressional authority, thus negating the wishes of the people. That's exactly what Obama did when he loaned or gave $2 billion to Brazil for offshore drilling at the same time he refused to grant new drilling permits to Americans in the Gulf of Mexico or in the Atlantic Ocean.

One might say that it would be easy for a president to become a dictator, observes Ron Paul. An even greater reality is that our current Fed chairman, Ben Bernanke, is already a dictator. Who needs another one?

Funding of the CIA from private sources is well known. Their off-balance-sheet money comes from private businesses, banks, and illegal drug trade. Paul believes the president's Working Groups On Financial Markets can manipulate markets and profit from it—all off budget.

The Exchange Stabilization Fund, the CFTC, the SEC and the Treasury, along with the Federal Reserve, can fund almost anything they desire. Ron Paul said it wasn't difficult to fund the secret wars in Afghanistan and Nicaragua in the 1980s.

Chapter Footnotes

Denson, John 2001. Reassessing The Presidency: The Rise of The Executive State And The Decline of Freedom. Auburn, AL: Mises Institute.

Fisher, Louis. 2004. Presidential War Power. Lawrence University Press of Kansas.

Morely, Felix. Freedom and Federalism. Indianapolis: Liberty Fund.

Savage, Charlie. 2008. Takeover: The Return of The Imperial Presidency and The Subversion of American Democracy. New York: Back Bay Books.

19

Foreign Aid

At one time Republicans opposed all foreign aid

Today, the debate is who should receive Aid. But there are Tea Party conservatives who want to eliminate all foreign aid. Did you know that we still give foreign aid to China? Here is a country that on or before 2040 is projected to replace the United States not only in Gross Domestic Product, but as some people say, it's armed forces will challenge us for supremacy in the World.

What do you think? Does foreign aid benefit national security? This writer says no. It encourages a foreign policy that "leads to unintended consequences that come back to bite us." Is it our duty to help impoverished nations? No. If you are using your own funds, maybe you could argue differently. But these are American taxpayer funds and they ought to be considered sacred.

Foreign aid means taking money out of the hands of private people who should be free to say how their money is spent. What does Ron Paul say? "Allowing government...decisions on spending capital are always inferior to private companies and people deciding how their money should be spent."

Foreign aid never works to achieve the stated goal of helping the poor of the nations. Politicians in receiving countries decide how the money is spent. In poor countries foreign aid becomes a tool for maintaining political power. This is why Congressman Paul and I believe that churches should not give aid directly to foreign governments as is necessary if you're dealing with Arab countries.

The same thing is true in dealing with the Muslim Brotherhood. It receives material and commodities from anyone and plaster across the pallets the Muslim Brotherhood name to make it look like they came from the Brotherhood, helping the Muslim Brotherhood to become popular among the people.

Churches, despite excellent motives of giving, should not become pawns of dictators, which the Muslim Brotherhood has become. If the underlying goal of the church is to pony up to the Brotherhood to receive a favor back, such as permission to proselytize their members, they are badly informed. That will never happen.

If the reason churches continue to give this way is to let the people know the source of the Christ-like love, that also will fail in repressed societies. The dictator or the Muslim Brotherhood, which sometimes is one and the same, will see to that. If it is merely to be kind and to accomplish the will of the Lord, it may or may not be successful because in Arab countries there is much greed, graft, envy, theft, and dishonesty about these goods. Many needy people are held up or not even given the goods because of the evil that resides in the hearts of the intermediary.

Since the Camp David Accords under President Jimmy Carter, Israel has received more than $100 billion and Egypt more than $70 billion from America. Both countries have become more dependent on the U.S. and less capable of taking care of themselves.

Peace may have come even without our money.

Spending foreign aid for weapons bought into the U.S. is common place and one reason conservative Republicans have been champions of foreign aid—it is good for our military-industrial complex.

Recipients then become reliable military allies and well armed.

Too often countries receiving our aid have turned against us. This is actually true in China's case. Also, hundreds of millions of dollars have been delivered through multi-liberal organizations such as the World Bank, International Monetary Fund, and the Federal Reserve. The Fed is allowed to make secret agreements with foreign governments, central foreign banks, and other international foreign institutions.

An audit of these agreements has never been allowed, according to Mr. Paul. Thus, it is impossible for us to know if the Fed participates in foreign policy decisions and strategy affecting American citizens.

Congressman Paul says that in November, 2010, the Fed was pressured to "cough up" information about its practices. "Many were shocked to discover that so much of the newly created money went to the biggest players in the banking industry and to foreign institutions.

"Foreign aid can be described as taking money from the poor in a rich country and giving money to the rich in a poor country."

20

Four Freedoms

The four freedoms refer to

Franklin D. Roosevelt's odious

Four Freedoms Speech of January 6, 1941

Franklin Delano Roosevelt not only wanted Americans to have these four freedoms, but, like it or not, he was going to give it to the world. As we have found in Iraq and Afghanistan, the world doesn't want our form of democracy. In fact, they reject it because they know if they embrace either a democratic republic or a democracy they will have to discard teachings of Mohammad and principles of Sharia Law which they so love.

The First Amendment Freedom of Speech everywhere in the world

The First Amendment Freedom of Religion everywhere in the world

Freedom From Want everywhere In the world

Freedom From Fear everywhere in the world

Referring to the first two freedoms, the Constitution says Congress shall write no laws referring to them. Ron Paul adds that if Congress cannot write such laws, neither can the judiciary and the executive branches of government

But what is odious is that Roosevelt changed this. He implied that enforcement was a federal matter. He also said he was mandating the phrase "everywhere in the world" to each of his "four freedoms."

This implied that world government would be the natural consequence of these words, "everywhere in the world." He claimed this would be the answer to dictatorship. But FDR didn't bother to say where he got the authority to accomplish this.

Dr. Paul believes that pursuing a policy of "freedom from want" is no less than announcing a license to steal.

Such a policy guarantees poverty for the masses and power to the government elite. To declare absence of want as a right mocks the notion that every person has a right to his or her life and a responsibility for it. "To describe the redistribution of wealth by an authoritarian government as a 'freedom' can only lead to socialist or fascistic schemes—of which we have seen many," Dr. Paul said.

Governments who want to expand their power cannot guarantee freedom from fear. Government bureaucracy begets fear—it doesn't eliminate it. That is how silly that statement is.

But Roosevelt said freedom from fear could be achieved by reduction of worldwide armaments to prevent aggression. But actions speak louder than words. As if he wanted war with Japan—which some people have argued—within seven months of his speech he stopped all oil shipments to Japan which helped lead to the bombing of Pearl Harbor.

Roosevelt maneuvered the U.S. into war. Ron Paul asserts the result was just the opposite from his stated goal. That was reduction of worldwide armaments to prevent aggression. Instead, the U.S. has become the largest producer and distributor of weapons of war in all of history. Do as I say, some parents tell their children, not as I do.

Eleanor Roosevelt saw to it that the Four Freedoms Declaration was included in the United Nation's Declaration of Human Rights. Its preamble reads: "Freedom from fear and want has been proclaimed as the highest aspiration of the common people."

Guaranteeing freedom from want and fear guarantees the destruction of liberty. We have been living with this declaration for seventy years; and our country and the world are more fearful and in greater need than ever, "facing a financial crisis of epic proportions."

Paul's answer to FDR is that "everyone's life is his own, and the fruits of his labors should be his as well."

This right to life and property comes naturally—freedom, agency, and liberty are God-given as well—from the creator, not from government.

Ron Paul said it: "The most that should ever be expected from government is to protect liberty."

The congressman is also right when he argues that "consenting for a greater role for government violates the moral defense of freedom." A majority of people can't give the liberties of others away. Government should protect the minority and prevent the majority from becoming the dictator by winning elections by majority vote. You can't generate freedom from want and fear. This false idea can destroy the concept of liberty.

The fear-want concept leads to terrible consequences. It means a person has a right to whatever he wants or needs and it can be obtained by robbing from those who produce. Freedom from want and fear opens a Pandora's box. Fear is a nebulous term. It can be artificially created.

Ron Paul reminds us that wants are endless and are unrelated to the concept of freedom. Is government to provide for any need and desire? It can't and it shouldn't.

Government never produces anything. Its only option would be to steal it from someone. Such governance would produce a system of big money and lobbyists, which deplorably, America has. Undermine the concept of rights and you destroy the basic premises underpinning society: private property, free choices, contracts, and sound money. Those are Ron Paul's ideas to which I subscribe wholeheartedly.

I fear for America. Most believe the people have a right to food, shelter, clothing, medical care, and jobs. This is misguided. It results from a misunderstanding of what freedom is all about.

Freedom from want can only be achieved by force at the sacrifice of liberty. Ask the Soviets how that worked out.

Compromise is not good if you are compromising basic values—especially if it's just to get re-elected. You might as well be compromising with the Devil. Compromise with liberals and progressives is an admission that government planning is better than private planning. That's why we have elections every two, six, and four years in America—to clean out the dead wood, those who have been in Washington so long that they can see nothing wrong with it. Ron Paul is one of the few exceptions to the rule for he is known for courageously standing up to corrupt politicians and he knows how to simply say "no."

The personal income tax was harmless enough at first. It started at one percent and applied only to the rich. But look at the size of the tax code today. Its 20,000 pages are Greek to most people—even to most members of Congress.

Ron Paul says that even the IRS agents cannot agree on the code's interpretation. Talk about being an obstructionist and not compromising. A one percent initial concession has been turned into a tax code that steals sixty percent of some peoples' income.

Payroll taxes are a huge burden to the poor. The IRS is looting everyone, crushing us all under the financial strain.

"All political energy for at least 100 years," said Congressman Paul, "has been directed toward increasing government power to determine who will receive the benefits. The result has been crumbs to the poor and an attack on the middle class, while Wall Street and the banks continue to benefit from the bailouts."

He suggests that only a clear understanding and protection of individual liberty can rescue us from the pending economic and political disaster. Our government and its leaders are continually manufacturing fear by invoking a current Hitler about to attack us.

It could have been Saddam Hussein, Mahmoud Ahmadinejad, the Taliban, the communists, al Qaeda, or whoever. This fear is necessary to get the public's support to fight unnecessary wars and support the military-industrial complex.

James Madison said it best: "War is the most dreaded enemy of liberty."

21

Global warming is dead

and now it's climate control

Congressman Paul doesn't believe in either. "The idea that governments can plan weather patterns for decades strikes me as the height of absurdity."

Paul believes that:

Many in the global warming camp simply do not like economic progress. They loath the internal combustion engine.

They are against pesticides, asphalt, oil, cars, meat, and modernity in all its forms. They long for a simpler time when there were only 500 million people living on earth because that is all that the food supply would sustain.

Like most Americans, Ron Paul believes that this attitude is creepy and dangerous. If taken seriously, he believes it could unravel economic progress and lead to suffering and death. Building up fear describes the biggest ploy of progressives. They create a problem and the electorate demands government save them. Then they jump in and offer silly solutions to the artificial problem they created. .

It's the oldest trick in the book. FDR used it when he wanted to get America involved in World War II. He sent out unguarded supply ships to Britain which were mysteriously sunk by what were supposed to be German U-Boats. Sometimes they were German vessels, but Roosevelt achieved his goal. America was sucked into the war. Likewise with Japan. We caused the Japanese to panic in the winter of 1941 when we deprived them of heating oil.

We broadened the war when the Japanese bombed Pearl Harbor. But that's only part of the story. First, Roosevelt placed an oil embargo on Japan and that angered them enough to attack.

"Artificial fear not only generates support, but demands that we pursue war policies, no matter how dangerous and ill-advised they may be."

Fear worked to make people fearful of a drastic market and economic collapse in America in 2008. That paved the way for the president to ram through Congress bailout of big banks and corporations and this was approved by a fearful Congress "that became convinced that an economic Armageddon was at our doorstep."

Paul and others believe the same kind of fear was used to propagandize Americans, raising to the extreme feelings that we were doomed. All the while, their goal was to socialize our nation and de-industrialize it. Congressman Paul kindly uses the phrase, "seemingly on purpose." This author is convinced, however, that it was intentional and that nothing is a coincidence.

"Radical environmentalism has systematically undermined the defense of free markets for decades, but especially in the past twenty years. Everything from early public school indoctrination to our media and Hollywood have created such a poisoned atmosphere of political correctness that any questioning or dissent on the science used to support the radical environmentalist position is ridiculed and written off as crazy talk." When in reality, it is the environmentalists—the global warming freaks— who are most often found to be the crazy ones.

This hysteria stopped all nuclear plant development for the past thirty years. This has caused higher prices at the pumps and higher prices for the energy we use in industry and in our homes.

Instead, these radical global warming kooks put all their marbles into government subsidized wind power, which is not, and won't be, competitive.

To replace one nuclear power generator you need windmills to cover an area the size of Connecticut. "Sensible green environmentalists are becoming aware of this and are taking a second look at Nuclear power."

Paul believes industrial growth in a free market is the only solution to poverty and hunger. He knows that the CO2 hysteria is a hoax. New regulations will massively increase poverty and hunger in the world and will hurt the environment.

This is true because factories that leave more efficient conditions and go to, say, China, are being pushed into third world countries where the cheapest form of fossil fuel is used.

Polluting one's neighbor's property, air, or water is contrary to market ethics and law. Trading permits to pollute—as President Obama would like us to do when he passes Cap and Trade—would not be considered. "Only central economic planners come up with schemes like this."

Paul says we must fight the environmentalists. If this were just an academic discussion it wouldn't matter that much, "but it has major ramifications; if the extremists are not refuted we will pay dearly for it and compound the economic crisis that we've already brought on ourselves."

Dr. Arthur B. Robinson, in his newsletter Access to Energy, and other scientists confirmed that climate change and temperature variations are related to sunspot activity and water vapor. "An increase in hydrocarbon use since 1940 has had no noticeable effect on atmospheric temperature, or on the trend of glacial length." He says there has been a 2 percent increase in hydrocarbons in the atmosphere the past 50 years but it is unrelated to temperature changes. Higher CO2 changes will cause plants to grow faster and larger with less water.

Paul uses good logic: "Man, over the centuries, became more civilized and, with technology, advanced and learned how to harness energy to protect us from the elements and at the same time raised our standard of living.

By using energy placed on earth for a purpose, we overcame the deadly natural elements of weather—heat and cold, wind and rain, floods and droughts.

People conquered the difficulties of persistent and unpredictable climate change, and now we're told we caused the problem we have successfully been able to overcome to a large degree.

22

Gun Control

Gun control is a political loser

Even the Democrats realize that. Ron Paul knows that they have been conspicuously silent on this issue for some time. There is declining public support for gun control. On the contrary, more states have adopted concealed carry programs. The National Rifle Assn. states that 24 states have adopted "shall issue" laws, replacing laws that prohibited carrying, or that issued carry permits on a very restrictive basis. The number of privately-owned guns has risen by about 90 million since 9/11.

The 9/11 terrorist attack and rising fears about security only made matters worse for gun control proponents. Millions of us have decided we can no longer depend on government to protect us. You can't remove guns from the people. Paul says the firearm technology exists. Take all the guns and the people will create more guns. "As long as there is metalworking and welding capability, it matters not what gun laws are imposed upon law-abiding people. Those who wish to have guns, and disregard the law, will have guns."

The Congressman adds that when you take guns from the people, you clear the path for violence. It makes aggression more likely. Paul doesn't believe in gun-free zones. If they worked, why does violence still exist in gun-free zones, such as at schools? Even if you don't like guns, you benefit from those who do. It is good that criminals believe they face an armed, rather than an unarmed, society.

Look at Switzerland where all citizens have guns and carry them. Aggressive behavior is not common. Nations that think this little country would be a pushover have another think coming. No one dare attack the Swiss.

Hitler showed us that a tragedy of gun laws is genocide. If a government is going to kill its people, it will have to disarm them first so they can't fight back.

Paul believes disarmament of people has to occur when trust of government is high. During the radical Obama administration, which until late February, 2012, has a very low approval rating of from 35 percent to 41 percent, this is not possible. If Obama's approval increases to sixty percent, watch out.

Our fifty-six founders knew that governments can change from good to bad overnight. Thus, they enacted the Second Amendment that authorizes citizens holding guns. They believed that an armed society was better than one unarmed, and they had the recent history of their own people defeating the greatest army in the world, the Brits who had invaded these shores. America is what it is today because of armed citizens.

Tyrants from Hitler to Mao to Stalin have sought to disarm their own citizens. They did so for the simple reason that an unarmed people are easier to control.

23

Hate Crimes

Belonging to a certain group or class of
people should not confer on them more rights
than those of the majority or the common citizen

To do this we re-enter an era where some people
could destroy another's property and hurt or kill
him, often without repercussion. For example, if
laws are not written to make it illegal for all people,
then you re-enact the era of the Ku Klux Klan. This
was a terrorist group that strung up black folks. The
first Klan flourished in the South in the 1860s,
then died out by the early 1870s. Members adopted
white costumes: robes, masks, and conical hats
designed to be outlandish and terrifying, and to
hide their identities.

It is no secret that these murderers were Democrats who opposed rights for the blacks. In later years, the Klan included Senator Harry Bird (D-V) and others who were revered by fellow Democrats, despite past association with the Klan.

The second KKK flourished nationwide in the early and mid 1920s and adopted the same costumes and code words as the first Klan, while introducing cross burnings. The third KKK emerged after World War II and was associated with opposing the civil rights movement and progress among minorities.

The second and third incarnations of the Ku Klux Klan made frequent reference to America's "Anglo-Saxon" and "Celtic" blood, harking back to 19th-century nativism and claiming descent from the original 18th-century British colonial revolutionaries. In all periods of the Klan, there are records of them engaging in terrorism. Historians debate how widely the tactic was supported by the membership of the second KKK.

In those days the power that was exercised and excused was used on blacks and perhaps against gay people. Paul reminds us that the only solution is to guarantee that all rights apply to all people equally—that all rights are individual rights and are unrelated to belonging to any particular group.

Too often we hear references to gay rights, minority rights, and women's rights, for example. All of which undermines the concept of individual rights.

Thought police is a concept that results when the law tries to determine the crime, using the idea that a crime can be judged by whether it was motivated by hate for certain groups.

If someone is robbed, raped, or killed, generally the penalty should be—but isn't— the same regardless of what the perpetrator was thinking at the time. (First degree murder demands malice aforethought. Without such, the penalty would be much less than death)

But judges have taken liberty to set the punishment based on what the criminal was thinking, and this not only cannot be done, it establishes bad precedence and criminal loopholes.

Hate crime legislation always comes up short in punishing the guilty person and promoting justice. It is classified only as collateral damage when American bombs kill innocent people, not a hate crime.

"Retaliation against Americans occupying a foreign country 7,000 miles from our homeland is called terrorism," said Paul, *"supposedly motivated only by ingrained and irrational hate."*

All too often the obsession with "political correctness" not only solves nothing, but governs whether a perverted view of equal justice will obtain.

24

Immigration

Why is immigration so emotionally charged?

It's a hot button because of huge economic considerations, violence and drugs, and our weak economy. All immigrants benefit liberals and Democrats more than they help the conservative cause. Illegal immigrants, right or wrong, are counted in the census, which statistically adds up to several congressional districts.

Texas gained four new seats after the 2010 census was completed. To a large degree, this was due to the Lone Star State's immigration policies, which are lax.

The economic and jobs reason fires up the electorate like none other. Immigrants take jobs from American working people. Federal law requires that the states pay for the medical and educational needs of these immigrants and some people are quite upset about part of their taxes going toward the illegal alien benefits when they don't pay taxes and they send all or most of their pay home to Mexico.

Ron Paul is a libertarian. He said that in a perfectly libertarian world, borders would be blurred and open. It would be like it is when someone wants to cross from New York to New Jersey or from California to Arizona. A passport is not required and practices in each state are quite similar.

Is Ron Paul a One World advocate? No, not in the sense as the United Nations, the hard core aggressive Muslims, and the notorious and predominantly big-bank-oriented Bilderberg Group envisions a one-world condition.

Paul explains: "The libertarians who argue for completely open borders for the free flow of goods and people fail to realize that a truly libertarian society would not necessarily be that open. The land and property would be privately owned and controlled by the owners (no government ownership of land), who would have the right to prevent newcomers from entering without their permission. There would be no government havens or welfare benefits and new immigrates would come only after a sponsor's permission."

Americans' greatest resentment comes from "government-mandated free services and a government-created unemployment crisis." He believes if we fix these two problems, it won't be necessary to find a scapegoat for our economic crisis.

Ron Paul advocates for a free and prosperous economy that looks for labor. He foresees a time when immigrant workers would be needed and welcomed. "This need could be managed by a generous guest worker program, not by illegal immigrants receiving benefits for the family and securing an easy route to permanent citizenship."

Today, immigrants are pawns of partisan political interests.

The dichotomy between protection from immigrants trespassing on the land of big businesses and farmers is glaring. For example, Dow Chemical has fences and private security guards. There are no trespassers, and if a problem arises, police are called.

"But if a rancher on our borders wants to stop trespassers on his land, he is forbidden to do so by the government," Paul said. Despite the poor policing job the Feds are doing, they don't even allow state officers to interfere.

Paul is aware that our borders are a battleground. There is a war going on. He is also up to date on drug trafficking from Mexico to the U.S. But he believes the problem is a consequence of "the ridiculous notion that drug prohibition is a sensible social policy."

"Everyone should know by now," he said, "that our current war on drugs makes no more sense than alcohol prohibition did in the 1920s." He believes that when you look at Afghanistan and their drug war problems, you can better understand the drug trade and corruption that is taking place right on our borders, threatening to be part of America. The huge profits that can be made are a significant incentive for corruption.

Plan One: Use the U.S. Army to round up the twelve million illegal aliens and ship them off.

Plan Two: Reward the lawbreakers, give them amnesty, and make them citizens. Thus insulting those who have patiently waited and obeyed immigration laws until their turn comes up to become U.S. citizens.

I am surprised to read that Ron Paul is not happy with Plan One. Or is he just being pragmatic in saying that is not going to happen? Paul says the Obama Administration lacks the determination and the resources to do this.

Others such as Mitt Romney, Michelle Bachman, and Herman Caine say complete the fence before you send those people home, and then stand by the rule of law in America and rigorously live the letter of the law and keep out foreigners who don't belong here. They changed their minds when someone suggested that it would cost ten-million dollars a mile.

Paul is afraid of splitting up families among some who have lived here a long time. He seems to say that a Good Samaritan approach to the problem would be to deal with each illegal on a case-by-case basis. One must remember that some of these people have lived in America longer than in Mexico. Many of them might not ever have lived in Mexico. Many might have lived there less time than in America and wouldn't be able to cope with living and working conditions in Mexico—if, indeed, they could find a job there.

One must say, however, that they knew they might get sent home at any time when the came here. All of the above is not the problem of the United States. Paul believes that the toughest part of giving these people any kind of amnesty is the message you are sending to other Latinos that they can come here, break the law, and the stupid Americans won't or can't send you home.

Many immigrants have great work ethics, even better than many Americans who were born here and who have chosen welfare rather than working hard and earning their own way.

Admittedly, Paul lacks the wisdom of King Soloman, but here's his plan:

Restore our country's economy to a healthy free market nation with sound money. Eliminate deficit-financed government. A vibrant economy will minimize the problems and produce a high demand for both domestic and immigrant labor.

Abolish the welfare state. People must be willing always to take a job—at whatever wages are available.

With free markets and private property, there will be a great need for immigration labor. Make it legal and attractive with a generous visitor work program. (Paul must have looked at the Utah immigration plan, because that's what it is purported to do).

Put more guards on the borders and enforce current law. Permit states to enforce the law; allow landowners to provide private property security assistance, and work with U.S. Border Control agents. Private landowners have a right to post "No Trespassing" signs on their property to enforce this.

Do not grant automatic citizenship to children of illegal aliens—those children who were born here on purpose or accidentally.

Stop all mandates on the states to supply free medical and free education to illegal aliens and their children.

Rick Perry and the Texas Legislature have created a real problem. Paul says, "The absurdity that south Texas schools are overburdened with Mexicans going back and forth over the border each day to our public school systems is resented by cash-strapped school districts."

Bilingualism should always be voluntary and not compelled by law. Don't punish companies or other third parties. They should not be required to enforce the immigration law, even if they happen to hire one of these individuals.

Also don't blame the Church for helping these people.

End the drug war. (I presume Paul means admit we lost and allow drug violations to go on, which is astounding if, indeed, this is what he means). "It's time to treat all drugs the way we treat alcohol and cigarettes, substances that kill far more than hard drugs do." (this is an astounding admission of failure of the U.S. and if Paul said this in one of his debates he would get booed off the stage, even if he later is found right in his assertion.)

Immigrants who can't be sent back across the border due to the magnitude of the problem should not be give citizenship. No amnesty should be granted. "Maybe a green card with an asterisk could be issued.

Those immigrants—legal or illegal—who incite violence or commit crimes of violence should be prosecuted and lose their right to stay in this country.

Police should not be prohibited from determining an individual's citizenship if the person is caught participating in a crime. This is far different from stopping people anytime and demanding they produce documents of legal status.

Paul admits that the above solution is far from perfect, but solutions to government-induced problems are never easy. He warns that the tighter we make our borders, with laws that keep people out, the more chance there will be for government abuse of its citizens. Just as instituting the Patriot Act has created a government that spies on its citizens in more ways than merely what is taken in a bag when you buy an airline ticket and go through the security check points.

25

Insurance

Having served for almost 40 years in insurance,

I sense Ron Paul's exceptional

insurance and banking moxie

In this chapter Dr. Paul debunks even the effort of socialists to say that anything offered by the government is insurance. Barak Obama's newest $840 million dollar stimulus bill was designed to create an infra structure bank, funded by taxpayer money—ten billion dollars each of the first two years of its operation. Some Washington bureaucrats err in saying it is only an instrument of insurance, a backup plan, and therefore it is harmless.

This so-called insurance bank, or infra structure bank, is designed to pay for roads, bridges, turnpikes, new highway construction, university buildings, airports, airport control towers, inland waterways, sewage disposal plants, electrical transmission, and anything else they can dream up. User taxes would pay for these facilities over thirty-five years. Nothing could possibly go wrong with those entities, could it? Don't be so naive. Project defaults, even in government, are legion. And who stands as the payer of last resort to bail everyone out? Taxpayers, you and I.

One of the problems with a government insurance company or a government bank is the overhead. It screams fraud and waste. Most people who know about insurance prefer gas taxes. Then they know that the money goes directly to the entity for which the tax is levied, not through several dipsy-do detours taking big bites out of the revenues for discretionary items not originally intended in the bill.

"Once government gets involved in providing insurance for any economic purpose, it no longer qualifies as insurance," observes Ron Paul.

"Insurance is about measuring risk and finding market opportunities to reduce the consequences associated with inescapable risk that exists as part of our lives."

Insurance is a broad enough subject to include bonding: surety (like contractor completion bonds); fidelity (honesty bonds); municipal bonds (that fund public building projects like offices, fair ground facilities, stadiums and mass transit); and structured finance bonds to pay for collateralized debt obligations. There are also Revenue Bonds, financing specific projects like a toll bridge or a highway.

This chapter is a primer for anyone wanting to better understand insurance in its several forms: life insurance; homeowners; auto; boat and yacht; boiler and machinery; docks and piers; commercial buildings and risks and bonding such as that listed above.

Congressman Paul correctly notes that you can't insure against risks that are illegal or that you, yourself, create: such as losing the lottery, against business failure, and against losing a sports match. That doesn't mean that there aren't people who will wager or bet on all of those unforeseeable events. But, then, that's called gambling, isn't it. Insurance is not gambling.

Why do we need underwriters? As Paul puts it, insurance is only profitable for both the insurer and the insured if risk is properly measured and priced. It takes competitive markets to find the proper price for insurance. Without certain indispensable things, insurance fails. Likewise, Socialism also fails because it lacks a competitive free marketplace, providing free market pricing,

"Government subsidized or regulated insurance will always fail in the same fashion, because there is a moral hazard embedded as part of its underlying structure: it is not properly priced according to the level of risk."

A moral hazard exists when an insurer covers a restaurant where the owner intentionally fails to clean out kitchen filters where grease accumulates, causing fires. It occurs when a gambling house lies to the underwriter about his employee who, unknown to the carrier, has robbed banks. These risks cannot be properly priced to the level of the risk. And, yes, specialized insurance does insure gambling houses, if not the act of gambling done there.

Ron Paul suggests that the government's definition of insurance is grossly misleading. "Social Security is not properly considered insurance." Neither are government-provided health benefits.

Nor is tax-funded flood insurance. "All of these programs are more accurately described as transfer payments. The question is why does America continue to bail out homeowners whose homes are inundated with flooding river water every two years? To receive payments from the government, it is supposed to be necessary for these people to leave known "flood plains" and rebuild elsewhere. But this provision is often poorly enforced.

In a like manner, it is contrary to logic for American taxpayers to continue to bail out the City of New Orleans every time this city floods. It is a city ten to sixteen feet below sea level, a flood waiting to happen. The chance for flood loss in New Orleans is a known factor. It is, therefore, not on the basis of any principle of insurance that we bail them out. What we do is give them politically expedient handouts.

What happens when the government is broke and can no longer offer handouts? The people do what they should have done long ago—they move their homes to higher ground.

Ron Paul has it right: "...the term "government insurance" is an oxymoron—a total contradiction. And that applies to all government 'insurance' programs."

One of the biggest problems today is misconception. Many believe that government is capable of insuring all of us against risks economic, both domestic and foreign. "Government has nothing to give to some, other than that which they steal from others."

Many in public educational institutions have perpetrated a lie—that government supervision is efficient and proper. The trend toward dependence on government solutions violates the restraints in the Constitution and ignores history's explicit record of authoritarian government's failure.

"If we follow the rules of limited government and personal responsibility, the issue of moral hazard would be dramatically reduced to those who commit fraud to insurance companies instead of endorsing an entire political and economic system based on immoral behavior that has given us our economic crisis and a foreign policy of perpetual war."

Ron Paul says trust in government authoritarians has appeal in America. But it is the foundation of moral hazards. Many Democrats say average people aren't smart enough to take care of themselves. "Those who promote the virtues of government interference in our lives and economy do it with a proud arrogance, convinced that average people can't and won't do what's in their best interest."

Above all, convince our youth to vote for change in Washington. It doesn't matter which of the Nine Republican candidates wins the nomination and is pitted against Obama or another Democrat if he decides not to seek re-election in November, 2012. Every one of them could run this country better than Obama has run things.

But if you want a candidate who really understands things, vote for Dr. Ron Paul. He is a real conservative, not a neocon or a moderate like most of the GOP hopefuls. He is the smartest candidate out there, the only one who has a doctor of medicine, and the only true conservative who can make America prosperous again in the shortest amount of time.

"Most conservatives, along with many liberal and moderates, support militarism and world occupation, which makes it convenient to believe that military spending is a patriotic jobs program. They want to protect freedom and create jobs—great politics, especially if the jobs end up in certain members' districts."

Try to eliminate from your thinking and that of the youth of our country, the idea that all conservatives think alike. They don't. Most who call themselves conservatives are big warfare proponents. They are not like Ron Paul. Military Keynesianism is every bit as dangerous as domestic Keynesianism.

"Some jobs are created to build bombs and missiles, but only at the expense of other jobs that would make better use of capital." In Paul's opinion, "Having so many weapons, especially those offensive in nature, only encourages the deeply flawed and immoral policy of 'preventive' wars." In reality that is just another phrase for aggression.

26

Keynesianism

It was the ideas of J.M. Keynes that got

America in deep trouble

The Democrat progressives continue to use that kind of "stimulus" and "bailout" mentality in a failed attempt to release America from the economic depression that they created.

Keynes's prescription for getting us out of the depression of the 1930s had been around long before John Maynard Keynes arrived on the scene, but his name keeps popping up whenever people speak of government stimulus.

Inflation, price controls, and government controls have been known for thousands of years. Professor

Ludwig von Mises's explanation for Keynes's notoriety is that those who already practiced interventionist techniques of economy believed that Keynes provided them with a scientific knockout punch—a scientific explanation and rationale for doing what governments wanted to do anyway.

Government intervention became popular not for its validity—and certainly not because it worked—but because an actual social scientist-like economist endorsed it in the 1930s.

Dr. Paul believes that the disastrous shape of the economy in the 1930s provided the fear needed to intimidate people into accepting promises of the New Dealers while ignoring their loss of liberty.

FDR, the great anti-fear advocate, created fear and "worked to generate more of it."

Our current president, Barak Obama, is a disciple of Keynes. He is a central government planner who believes all problems can end with government intervention. The sorry problem is that all economic problems are either made worse by government or started by government.

What was it about the failure or collapse of the Chinese and the Soviet Union style of top down government and radical economic interventionism that liberals in Washington didn't get?

It is ironic that in an age of free markets—to which China and Russia have eagerly and successfully embraced—a U.S. president wants to return America to the Dark Ages. Wants to re-plough the field and turn over solid economic soil that worked in the past in exchange for failed philosophies of socialistic and communistic countries, concepts that did not work.

Didn't Ronald Reagan teach us anything about our economic system?

The answer? Apparently not, at least not to the communist reformers in America. But the foreign communists—China and Russia—got the message. They are much the better for it today while America's economy spits and sputters with one percent growth in GDP at the time of this writing (September 29, 2011) and the jobless rate stagnates just under ten percent with no help in sight except a losing big government strategy on the part of progressives. If you believe the government, our jobless rate is now 8.2 percent. I never take carte blanche government figures.

"Spending on bailouts, propping up mal-investments, borrowing, and inflating the currency cannot produce sound economic growth," said Congressman Paul. "Debt finally consumes the fictitious wealth built on sand that deceived the politicians, Main Street, and Wall Street into believing that real economic growth was occurring.

"Government borrowing and spending is not the solution; it is the problem." Producing and saving is the source of sound economic growth, a policy Keynesians readily decry."

Ron Paul said The Federal Reserve System is at the bottom of the progressive's deception. "Without a Federal Reserve to accommodate deficit spending, through monetary inflation, huge deficits would be virtually impossible. The idea that wealth without productive effort is possible is a Keynesian myth. It is this myth that deceives the Fed into believing it can create capital with the click of a computer and reject the notion that true capital can only come from production and savings."

Paul believes ordinary citizens have aided in the myth. Until 2011, our households spent too much. Now, however, we are awakening to the probability of the economy not coming back, at least not this year, 2011, and maybe not next year, 2012. People are still traveling, but they are vacationing closer to home. They have tightened their belts and are preparing food storage and increasing their rate of savings. Though it is hard to know where to put our savings, since small and large banks could fold up during the coming hard, hard times of this double-dip recession which this writer calls a depression.

Government stimulus programs, "paid for with deficits and money creation, become an economic narcotic addiction. The longer the dependency lasts, the greater the dosage required to alleviate temporarily the unwelcome symptoms of the necessary correction."

Paul is convinced that the message that the markets is sending today is that the age of Keynesian central economic planning is over. Spending is not a panacea, borrowing is stupid economics, government cannot solve our problems, Keynesianism has failed, and deficits do matter.

Reject the pie-in-the-sky promises of Keynes, reject the authoritarian goals of welfare and warfare, and accept that the role of government is limited and must be based on honest money.

When you see a youthful-looking Barak Obama clowning it up before ten thousand students at schools like North Carolina State as he did on CSPAN on September 14th, 2011, understand one thing: these Wolfpack students are voters and they are not currently motivated by truth because their liberal professors have filled their heads with political garbage. Go out of your way to speak to them, logic with them, convince them of the errors of Obama's past. And the errors of the socialistic and progressive regime in Washington

Above all, conservatives must control the Senate and the White House. Convince our youth to vote for conservative change in Washington.

It doesn't matter which of the Nine Republican candidates wins the nomination (as long as his last name is Paul) and is pitted against Obama or another Democrat if he decides not to seek re-election in November, 2012. Every one of them could run this country better than Obama has run things.

But if you want a candidate who really understands things, vote for Dr. Ron Paul. He is a real conservative, not a neocon or a moderate like most of the GOP hopefuls. He is the smartest candidate out there, the only one who is a doctor of medicine, and the only true conservative who can make America prosperous again in the shortest amount of time.

"Most conservatives, along with many liberal and moderates, support militarism and world occupation, which makes it convenient to believe that military spending is a patriotic jobs program. They want to protect freedom and create jobs—great politics, especially if the jobs end up in certain members' districts."

Try to eliminate from your thinking, and that of the youth of our country, the idea that all conservatives think alike. They don't. Most who call themselves conservatives are big warfare proponents. They are neo-cons. They are not like Ron Paul. Military Keynesianism is every bit as dangerous as domestic Keynesianism.

"Some jobs are created to build bombs and missiles, but only at the expense of other jobs that would make better use of capital." In Paul's opinion, "Having so many weapons, especially those offensive in nature, only encourages the deeply flawed and immoral policy of 'preventive' wars." In reality that is just another phrase for aggression.

27

Lobbying

How Do We Deal With The Lobbying?

Here's a thumbnail sketch about the problem and just how crucial it has become:

Petitioning the U.S. or any state government—often called lobbying—is protected by the First Amendment. "Congress shall make no laws respecting...the right of the people ...to petition the government."

Petitioning is a legitimate right.

Congress and the executive branch—can be petitioned.

Who are the American lobbies or special interests?

Drug companies

Medicine

Insurance

Military-industrial cabal

Foreign lobbyists

Big Farming

Big Auto Makers

Unions

Screen Actors Guild

American Law Association

Big Banking

Money influences votes in Congress. Big money influences votes in a big way. Today, corporations can give an unlimited amount of money to a candidate via a PAC, a political action committee.

The question is how can lobby abuse be eliminated? Answer: put less on the table for corporations and other special interests to purchase. Ron Paul's answer is to shrink the federal government to its proper size. It should not be involved overwhelmingly in "every domestic and international economic transaction. Since Barak Obama has come to power, the White House has added hundreds of rules and regulations. For example, now the ATF, Alcohol, Tobacco, and Firearms department, has started regulating Tuffy pads, those steel wool things we used to clean the kitchen. Someone told them they would make an excellent muffler of sound, or a silencer on a gun.

Similarly, you can't buy a fourteen-inch shoelace anymore without the ATF regulating the manufacturer of shoelaces. Some enterprising bloke showed them that a loop could be tied on each end of the shoelace. One end would pull back the hammer of a gun and the other would be held by a person's thumb or a finger, effectively making possible the discharge of that gun in rapid-fire fashion, just like a machine gun.

If President Obama has his way, before long you won't be able to buy any American product that does not carry the weight of regulatory review's big surcharges. Is it any wonder America can't compete in a worldwide marketplace? Any wonder that U.S. jobs are being shipped abroad?

Paul believes proper sizing of government is "not going to happen any time soon" without a true conservative in the White House.

Solutions?

1. **Require an amendment to the Constitution.** But Congress isn't the main problem, it's the president we're afraid of. Governor Rick Perry of Texas had an idea. Cut the national legislative session down to two months. I'm surprised that

Ron Paul didn't come up with that, but, again, Congress is not the current problem. If Congress was in recess ten months of the year, President Obama would merely rule by executive order. Then we would have a complete dictatorship on our hands and Congress would have to rush back to Washington to impeach the bounder.

2. Lower the president's term limits from two to one—one four-year term. Absolutely no re-election. I can hear the Democrats wailing: "Oh, no. You can barely get things going in four years." That's right. That's the point, we don't want these prideful executives to get anything going. They've done enough damage already.

That would release some of the executive office's steam. It would make his bulldozer misfire, shortening the campaigns and discouraging special interests from forking out the big bucks on any one candidate. Naysayers would argue that it would destabilize government. I believe it needs a lot of destabilizing. It has really gone off the wrong end, creating a socialist-Marxist nation out of a once free country

Lobbyists exercise immorally outrageous power. Dr. Paul does not believe term limits would solve anything, but I (Don White) do. But how can we guarantee that the replacements will do anything different? My plan could backfire. Knowing their time is limited, Congressmen and the president could put on racing shoes, quickly passing big-spending bills as fast as possible, with little time for debating the issues.. But that's the point. If there are enough conservatives in Washington, these high binders would be totally ineffective. But, when faced with the need to pass something important, their hands might be tied.

A third option: Congressman Paul says all we can do is send to Washington only those independent souls who can resist the temptation to "blend in with the crowd."

He sys there is tremendous pressure for new members to be team players. Idealism is not well received in D.C. Committee assignments come with team playing. Aloofness gets the new guy isolation.

Fourth, maybe we should abolish the seniority system and eliminate:

Temptations:

Accepting favors

Vote trading

Taking government money for projects at home

Newbie's are told they must serve their masters or employers (defined in D.C. as government) or find a new job.

It is difficult to find men and women who can resist the pressure of their peers and receive derision.

America Needs:

An educational revolution at home.

We must convince the masses that their interests are best served by providing liberty and sound economic policies rather than largesse.

Congressman Paul believes the revolution is best expressed in the Tea Party Movement. It is a sign that the disenfranchised are angry enough over the bailouts that their political action will bring about change in Washington. With better people and placing proper pressure on those already there to break the grips that the special interest lobbyists have over the system.

Ron Paul believes that a lot of pressure to break lobbyists power will come when the country's bankruptcy is shown in real grief and deprivation to the people.

"Maybe we can then reform the system," he said.

I say it won't come any more by a former lobbyist like Newt Gingrich than from a community organizer like Obama. People ripe in iniquity cannot reform anything. Though Gingrich says he can because he has converted to the Catholic Church, that he has seen the light and is a new man, I can't help but believe that this is merely a front for his nefarious past and true ideals.

Dr. Paul says once people recognize that demanding more from a government that is failing to fulfill its promises is futile. When the process unwinds, people will be forced to become more self-reliant.

28

Marriage

Proposition Eight In California

Ron Paul said that despite the fact that most people who want to get married don't argue about having to get a marriage license, the requirement generates heated disagreements and unnecessary problems.

He believes that if government wasn't involved, there would be no controversy over the definition of marriage. He was talking about California Proposition Eight. Gays lost that battle and immediately turned to violence, vandalizing temples, churches, and other church property.

Gays and Lesbians should appreciate and vote for Ron Paul. While other candidates say they are for the rights of Gays and all other people, only Ron Paul actually walks the talk. For example, read his words:

"Why should the government give permission to two individuals to call themselves married? In a free society, something that we do not truly enjoy, all voluntary and consensual agreements would be recognized. If disputes arose, the courts could be involved as in any other dispute."

Under our system, he believes the federal government was granted no authority over this issue. Congressman Paul would change the debate and turn it into a First Amendment rights debate, the right of free speech. "Everyone can have his or her definition over what marriage means, and if an agreement or contract is reached by the participants, it will qualify as a civil contract if desired."

Paul believes both sides want the government to force the other into submission. One side shows no tolerance to the other, while the other want the government to mandate their social acceptance "even though this is impossible for law to achieve." The primary goal of gays is spousal benefits. Paul believes this becomes an economic redistribution issue—a problem that would not be found in a truly free society.

There would be no problem if Gays were like the Amish, living off by themselves, minding their own business, not trying to penetrate normal society with their lifestyle dogma. But they are not. They want acceptance. And that includes being den masters or scoutmasters of non-gay scouts; being school teachers; having rights of adoption; rearing children in their homes; indoctrinating their adopted children to gay precepts and practices; and spreading their lifestyles throughout the country. Ecclesiastical opponents see this as an affront to normalcy and to a wholesome, God-principled atmosphere for children to grow up in. They point to sodomy and other Gay sexual acts as a hit on the very foundation civilization.

In all cases, gay people want government to force "equal" treatment. Gays, somehow, liken their treatment in society to what the black population endured before the Civil Rights Act was passed by Congress in the 1960s. Barak Obama's 2011 elimination of "Don't Ask, don't tell" in the military was seen by them as a monumental victory for gay rights.

If this were a truly free society, Dr. Paul believes agreements would solve the problem. But he doesn't see that on the horizon soon. Paul posits that creating Social Security accounts could be one answer. Then those proceeds could be passed on to family survivors, and people could name whomever they wanted to be their beneficiary, just as with private insurance policies.

Paul says Gay marriage is a state issue. Currently there are twelve states that recognize common-law marriage. No license is required. He doesn't think the issue deserves a constitutional amendment or government intervention. They serve no useful purpose. More tolerance and a lot less government in our lives is needed to avoid this "emotionally charged" debate.

"When we no longer believe that civilization is dependent on government expansion, regulating excesses, and a license for everything we do, we will know that civilization and the ideas of liberty are advancing."

29

Medical Care

Unfortunately, most People Believe they

Have A Right To Medical Care

While Ron Paul concedes that most Americans believe they have a right to medical care, it is an intellectual error. It will destroy the good in our system, replacing it with a system that is terrible for everyone. Why? Because the "supposed right to medical treatment can only be guaranteed at others' expense."

Free medical care is a massive wealth transfer. Because it is so massive, it can only be accomplished by force. Oppressive bureaucracy is its byproduct. Over utilization of resources will be its droppings, and technological stagnation and inevitable rationing and deprivation will be its terrible end result.

When someone goes to a doctor or a hospital today he and the medical facility are hindered by government policies. That's because of forty years of government interference in the process. Dr. Paul cites regulations, inflation, tax laws, and federal mandates to provide care through corporate HMOs, interference in providing insurance, massive subsidies, and licensing. "All have played a negative role in the delivery of medical care in the United States."

Paul compares government's hubris for medical regulation to what it would be like if it took responsibility for guaranteeing that every man, woman, and child had a cell phone. What if government called *it* a right and justified it for national defense purposes? "It would have been a nightmare. Quality would have never improved, prices would be sky high, and distribution lousy. But we now have affordable cell phones and the prices will continue to drop as more and more competition is encouraged by the market."

Take a look at the high costs of medical treatment. Dr. Paul blames government interference for the fact hospitals can charge $1,000 for a toothbrush and get paid for it. He said the Department of Defense pays $700 for a $5 hammer.

"It's the nature of government to produce low-quality products and services at extremely high prices. Socialist, bureaucratic, and interventionist economic systems inevitably injure most of the people who are supposed to be helped, and at a very high cost."

Why Medical Inflation Soars

Ron Paul examines why costs continue to soar for America's medical industry, while dropping due to competition in cell phones, TVs, and computers. He looks at the problem from a doctor's point of view and proclaims that Medicare and Medicaid are bankrupt, unattainable programs under current conditions. What are the conditions? He blames managed care and forty-five years of government interference for the problem.

It is understandable that a medical provider would be unhappy with managed care. But from the author's perspective, it is not the source of any problems, merely an inept response by insurance professionals to corral excessive costs and medical charges. Doctors and hospitals charge way too much for their services and blame government regulations. Insurance companies' response was justified. If the doctors had to charge outrageous prices, the ultimate payer, the people, who are represented by government, decided to lower those charges by a law change called managed care. Paul's angst as a doctor is understandable, however, because if he and other health care providers had their way they wouldn't have to charge so much.

Editor's note: The following is a true story from a man named Frank.

"After taking my daughter to an Orlando Hospital recently I totally disagree with Paul's assessment. She was injured when a tennis racked hit her in the arm, creating a welt but no fracture. She was charged more than a three thousand dollars for less than five minutes of emergency room care."

Here's another sad note about doctors and hospitals in America from Julius:

"In 2005 when our car was broadsided in an intersection, my wife was taken to the wrong hospital by the ambulance driver, probably on purpose. She spent an hour there and incurred bills for x-rays but no treatment and was released with a six thousand-dollar bill and a lame apology that she needed intensive care and that this hospital didn't offer it. All the while she is in extreme pain without medication, with one of my kids overhearing a doctor say the delay is okay because she isn't going to make it. We got back into the ambulance and they took her to the Orlando Regional Medical

Center where she stayed for four days and incurred a bill of $60,000. She needed to stay for a couple of weeks or so, but our bank account and insurance prohibited it. In other words, she came home before recovering. She slept upright in a living room chair because for several weeks we couldn't get a hospital bed to our home."

There was something morally wrong with the performance of two Orlando, Florida hospitals. Both Frank and Julius were convinced that services rendered were worth nothing like the amounts charged.

"After four days," said Julius, "we found they had mal-practiced on my wife. They had not treated a lacerated lung that, by the time we became aware of the problem, was no longer practical to operate on without grave and painful repercussions for her. So, even today, she essentially has only one lung thanks to the poor doctor services in those Florida hospitals."

This author asked Julius if he sued for malpractice? He said: "No, and maybe we should have but we didn't. I didn't have the heart to put her through more torment on top of the near death trauma she had just experienced. She was so close to death. Involving her with attorneys and the courts would solve nothing. Suing would not have helped her physically, but would only add to her pain and inconvenience."

When I mentioned what Dr. Paul had to say about the doctor-hospital situation in America, they were both adamantly disappointed with their hospitals. Julius said, "Thank Dr. Paul for his opinion, but our experience has shown that medical providers often fail to perform, and in our minds are a big part of the problem, not innocent bystanders." Julius said his wife was a nurse and that they had been around hospitals and doctors a lot and had seen it first hand.

So what caused America's medical problem? Dr. Paul blames lack of authentic price competition and seems to completely absolves the medical profession.

He compares it with what he believes is price competition in car insurance. The difference is that government has placed many mandates on health insurance, where car insurance bought and paid for by people comes with a cafeteria of coverage choices. People can choose to add or drop collision, comprehensive, and medical payment coverage as they wish. The only mandated coverage is a state imposed minimum liability amount to cover other people in case you, the insured, become liable in an accident.

Those minimum coverage amounts are insanely low. Many states still have between ten thousand to twenty-five thousand dollars as the mandated liability limit—which won't pay for much these days.

Compare that to the stringent requirement government places on hospitals and doctors. It isn't a free marketplace, It is shackled by rules made up in Washington. This industry is strictly mandated as to what they can do and what they can't do. One must also remember that the Multi-Resonance Imaging (MRIs) screens cost hundreds of thousands—even millions—of dollars. There are also expensive CAT scan and X-ray machines and computers. Operating rooms are digitalized, with computers and operating tools that are state of the art. All of this equipment is amortized out, with costs associated with it included in each hospital bill.

Driving up the costs are the laws covering medical malpractice. Unlike Frank and Julius'es wives, many patients do sue doctors and hospitals. The threshold of blame is so low today that doctors have been forced to run every possible test, x-ray, and screen to stay out of jail or to avoid multi-million-dollar malpractice lawsuits. Ron Paul says defensive medicine is epidemic. That has driven up the cost of medical

treatment in America. Now states are passing laws limiting malpractice awards.

Congressman Paul believes legalizing contracts could go a long way to solving the problem. But, unfortunately, agreements between patients and doctors on limiting liability and establishing third-party arbitration often do not hold up in court.

Dr. Paul says antitrust laws prohibit doctors from working together to devise contracts for a no-fault type of insurance that would exclude the trial lawyers from ripping off the system.

Do we need new legislation? Yes, badly. But don't expect politicians like Barak Obama, Mitt Romney, Newt Gingrich, and Rick Santorum who have been bought off by the Big-Pharma and the legal professions to offer you any improvements.

Ron Paul refuses to take such money. Therefore, he can help us get out of this dilemma. George Bush tried for it and failed in 2008. Barak Obama is a big-attorney man, himself, so don't expect anything from him.

Tort reform remains a major policy objective of the Republican party which is consistently opposed by the democrats. It was a major part of the Bush Administration's domestic agenda. The 2008

Republican platform pledged to reform what was described as corruption in the civil litigation system. Democrats are basically in a defensive position on the issue, but Senate Republicans often oppose tort reform or drag their feet because they are either attorneys themselves or receive money for re-election from various bar association lobbies.

If America would abolish the 17th Amendment, America wouldn't have such powerful senate lobbies because senators would be elected by state legislatures and, therefore, not subject to so much vote buying as currently exists in Washington.

State Laws Limiting Awards

Researchers at the Agency for Healthcare Research and Quality (AHRQ) have examined the impact of different kinds of State laws in a number of previous studies. This study examines the impact of State legislation that caps damage awards in malpractice cases on decisions of physicians about where to practice medicine.

Twenty-four States now have laws that limit damage payments in malpractice cases. Most of these laws limit the amounts paid for non-economic damages (e.g., pain and suffering) but a few limit both economic (e.g., medical expenses and lost wages) and non-economic damages. A national debate currently rages on the desirability of extending caps on malpractice damage awards to all States, and President Bush's proposal to cap payments for non-economic damages in medical malpractice cases at $250,000 went nowhere.

Supporters of legislation to cap damages in malpractice cases maintain that it reduces malpractice premiums and helps insure an adequate supply of physicians. They also assert that escalating, multi-million-dollar jury awards are driving malpractice premium increases and that capping damage awards for pain and suffering helps restrain the rate of increase. Without such a law the loss of affordable medical malpractice insurance for physicians could eventually lead to the loss of affordable, accessible health care.

Other government-sponsored insurance over which progressives are salivating:

Food insurance

2) Med Insurance for preconditions

3) Job insurance

4) College paid by government

Our shameless Occupy Wall Street protesters want hard-working taxpayers to pay for their college debt. What next? Cradle to grave coddling? They and the coeds who want free

condoms should be rounded up and shipped off to Cuba. Their intent seems to be to destroy America.

Free mass transit

6) Rent and housing subsidies

You realize that there are many ways government can provide insurance and services. Mass transit is a trap for most people. At first glance it may appear appealing until you research the topic and find that these systems in most areas of the country are a financial boondoggle because the cost-ride percentage is too great to justify the expense. But once government invests in free rides, forever the people will pay the taxes even if the system is unsuccessful, all the while realizing the public prefers by large numbers to drive their own cars than to ride with a bunch of disparate people to their stop-and-go, round-about destinations.

Dr. Paul said once insurance companies are required to pay for pre-conditions, it is no longer insurance—it's a social welfare mechanism and will end up bankrupting insurance companies…"or they will be bailed out by a government subsidy, further bankrupting the government. So far, no one has mandated insurance companies to sell fire insurance to a person whose home is on fire, or insurance on a beach house once the hurricane is a few miles offshore. Most people understand this, but for some reason they refuse to draw the analogy to medical insurance.

Ron Paul wants insurance-type rating for motorcyclists, smokers and over-weight hypertensives. "Why should those who have better health habits pay more to take care of those who don't?"

Paul also would:

* Make medical insurance available <u>across state lines</u>

* Stop medical insurance from <u>covering first-dollar expenditures</u>

* Reverse the system of pre-paid <u>services dictated by government rules</u>

* End managed care. He believes that <u>price control leads to shortages.</u>

* Provide incentives for patients and <u>providers to keep prices down</u>

A government system of anything has a nearly perfect record of failure, whether it's stopping war, preserving liberty, guaranteeing sound money, or generating economic prosperity.

Paul says in obstetrics the doctor is blamed for all bad outcomes regardless of fault and held responsible for any problems developing for twenty-one years. He suggests an insurance policy for nine months. Delivery would be paid for by the doctor and the patient to compensate for any bad outcome. He believes this is a policy that could evolve. Trial lawyers, eat your hearts out!

Tax credits should be offered for all medical care costs. That includes insurance for care as well as for problems of shared liability. Paul compares this to the way auto fender-benders are handled. They don't require a trial to determine the degree of injury, benefits and fault.

There must be more competition for people entering the medical field. He states that licensing strictly limits the number who can provide patient care. "Many of these problems trace to the Flexner Report of 1910, which was financed by the Carnegie Foundation and strongly supported by the AMA. Many medical schools were closed and the number of doctors was drastically reduced."

Dr. Paul claims the motivation was to close schools that catered to women, minorities, and especially homeopathy. We continue to suffer from these changes. They were designed to protect physicians' income and promote allopathic medicine over the more natural cures and prevention of homeopathic medicine.

We need to remove any obstacles for people seeking holistic and nutritional alternatives to current medical care. We must remove the threat of further regulations pushed by the drug companies now working worldwide to limit these alternatives. True competition in the delivery of medical care is what is needed, not more government meddling.

The threat isn't just from Democrats:

Obama's reforms are very similar to reforms pushed by the Republicans over the decades. The Republican Party under Eisenhower established the Department of Health, Education, and Welfare in the 1950s.

Nixon signed managed care ERISA laws in the early 1970s. This followed a decade of Democrats implementing their Medicare and Medicaid programs with strong Republican support.

Reagan expanded medical transfer payments. Prescription drug programs were passed by George Bush and a Republican Congress. Republicans shout "socialized medicine" as they become the nominal opposition of Obama Care.

Medical care has been taken over by corporations.

We have a form of corporatism veering on fascism.

We all know about the military-industrial complex. But what about the medical-industrial complex?

Regardless of party, corporate special interests are protected.

This involves medical management companies, hospitals, the AMA, drug companies and insurance companies.

Concern for patients is a smokescreen, as these entities lobby in Washington for their own interests. Corporations, unions, and governments stand between the patients and their doctors regardless of motivation.

The quality and cost of medical care will never be improved by forcing on the American people greater debt-financed involvement in medical care. Medicare and Medicaid are already bankrupt. Creating a new trillion-dollar system will only hasten the day of reckoning.

30

Monetary Policy

An Unchecked Central Bank

Ron Paul wrote the book *End the Fed.* On or off the campaign trail, he is constantly talking about the evils inherent in having an "unchecked" central bank. There is a lot of checking on expenditures that takes place in other areas of government. The U.S. Constitution (Article 1, section 9, clause 7) states that "…no money shall be drawn from the Treasury, but in Consequence of Appropriations made by Law; and a regular Statement and Account of Receipts and Expenditures of all public Money shall be published from time to time."

Because of this language, when Woodrow Wilson signed this into law in 1913 he purposely excluded presidential and Congressional purview from Fed business. Paul believes that section of the

Constitution needs to be changed to allow government (Congress and the President) authority to completely eliminate or limit Fed spending. He has spoken also of actually ending the Fed, the title to his book.

In 2011 he and his son, Senator Rand Paul, introduced bills in the House and Senate to allow auditing of the Fed.

Control Washington exerts on appropriated non-Fed spending

Each year, the President of the United States submits his budget request to Congress for the following fiscal year. The Budget and Accounting Act of 1921 requires a budget. During the Barak Obama era, much to the consternation of the public, there has been no budget. Obama is in violation of the law, but no one seems to do anything about this blatant disregard of U.S. law. The longer he gets away with it, the more succeeding presidents will rely on his precedent and the more liberals will assault and debase the U.S. Constitution which requires that laws be followed. Otherwise, why have Congress pass a law? I think you're getting the point. Otherwise, why have a congress? Who needs Congress if they and their laws are totally ignored—especially by the very one who is responsible to administering all laws? If the executive branch is free to disregard laws it disagrees with, you don't have a republic, you have a dictatorship. This is ample ground for impeachment.

Several government agencies from time to time do provide budget data on prospective bills. These include the Government Accountability Office (GAO), the Congressional Budget Office, the Office of Management and Budget (OMB) and the U.S. Treasury Department..

The CBO publishes *The Budget and Economic Outlook* in January, which is typically updated in August. It also publishes a *Monthly Budget Review*. I've never understood how they can do this without an actual budget to account for. The OMB, which is responsible for organizing the President's budget that should be presented in February, typically—when there is a budget—issues a budget update in July. The GAO and the Treasury issue *Financial Statements of the U.S. Government*, usually in December following the close of the federal fiscal year, which occurs September 30.

There is a corresponding *Citizen's Guide*, a short summary. The Treasury Department also produces a *Combined Statement of Receipts, Outlays, and Balances* each December for the preceding fiscal year, which provides detailed data on federal financial activities.

Historical tables within the President's "Budget" (OMB) is meant to provide a wide range of data on federal government finances. Many of the data series begin in 1940 and include estimates of the President's Budget for 2009– 2014. Yet during that same time period, in 1913, Congress and the President Woodrow Wilson voted for two abominable bills: the **Progressive Income Tax** and the establishment of a central bank called the **Federal Reserve System**.

Unfortunately, at that time and at no time since has Washington seen fit to audit the Fed. We should start talking about impeachment proceedings for the leadership in the House and Senate. Maybe we could spur some action. Maybe, then, we would get some teeth in a bill that would require a Federal Reserve System audit. It's our money, but few—except Ron and Rand Paul—seem interested in handling government as a business would. That is, require budgets, oversight, and proper accounting of funds to be spent and those spent in the dark of night when no one's looking. America must be asleep. Otherwise, we'd be hearing of broad protests involving the poor job our lawmakers are doing of running this nation.

American lawmakers have almost no information or control over what is actually spent by the Fed, the collection of loans made by the Fed, or names of recipients of this money—which is taxpayer money borrowed in the form of Treasury Bills which are purchased by countries like China and by private people and corporations.

We have heard that often the Fed has loaned or given money to foreign countries, and of course that is without government authorization. When the last supposed stimulus to help Americans find jobs was made by the Fed, it was split many ways, but one-third of it found its way to foreign shores. However, in late November, 2011 the Fed announced it was loaning Europe **$600 Billion** of our children's and grandchildren's money. Few Americans are happy about that. That is because they have so little information and understanding about Fed activities other than knowing that the 12 Fed Commissioners led by Fed Secretary Ben Bernanke are progressives, extremely liberal with our money, and they are of the Keynesian ilk who believe in spending government out of a financial crisis. Well, how did that work out during the last financial crisis? It didn't. And it never does, though they never seem to learn the lesson that if you as a citizen can't spend your way out of bankruptcy, why in the world does the government believe it can do so?

Ron Paul recently referred to a fine book called The Law by Frederek Bostiac. . It has to do with the ideal that the government can have no more rights than the individual represented by government. If it does, that government is too big and confiscatory, it steals from you because you no longer can control what it does. It is despotic and must be cut and ended or you will dwindle in prosperity and that's exactly where we're at.

The Federal Reserve doesn't care. It is all-powerful over your children's money. It controls the three tools of monetary policy—open market operations, the discount rate, and reserve requirements. The Board of Governors of the Federal Reserve System is responsible for the discount rate and reserve requirements, and the Federal Open Market Committee is responsible for open market operations. Using the three tools, the Federal Reserve influences the demand for, and supply of, balances that depository institutions hold at Federal Reserve Banks and in this way alters the federal funds rate. The federal funds rate is the interest rate at which depository institutions lend balances at the Federal Reserve to other depository institutions overnight.

Changes in the federal funds rate trigger a chain of events that affect other short-term interest rates, foreign exchange rates, long-term interest rates, the amount of money and credit, and, ultimately, a range of economic variables, including employment, output, and prices of goods and services.

Here are some of Dr. Paul's statements:

Talk about dangers of big government and loss of liberty is inadequate if the negative impact of the money managers is not addressed.

Avoiding the subject serves the interest of those who support expanding government welfare.

It also promotes an indirect way to pay for unpopular and unjust wars.

Money was once rooted in a scarce commodity known as gold and silver. It could not be manufactured by governments.

Since 1913 the Fed has printed new money, leading to instability and booms and busts.

Since 1871 the dollar has not been redeemable in anything but itself.

The dollar is nothing but a symbol.

There are no limits on the number of dollars the government and the Fed can create.

The result has been an expansion of the state, brutal and long inflation that has reduced our standard of living in deceptive ways.

What most people believe is that the Fed can get us out of jams. This is not true.

"The fact that the Fed was set up to be the lender of last resort, along with easy credit granted by the Fed, encouraged huge malinvestment and excessive debt," said Paul. "The gargantuan size of the derivatives market—a crisis not yet resolved—could not have occurred without a Federal Reserve and the moral hazard its policies generate.

"The Fed should have been blamed for most of our problems rather than credited with providing solutions to them."

Congressman Paul said the largest financial bubble in all of history has been caused by two things: 1) misplaced trust in the safety of government spending (the Keynesian spending theory) and 2) Federal Reserve easy credit.

He compares the Fed's Keynesian credo of spending your way out of trouble to a family in debt. "What sane person would advise a family member or a friend who was in over his head financially, in debt, and about to lose his home that the solution was to borrow more money and spend it and sign up for as many new credit cards as possible? It is ludicrous. In addition, he is told that it is not necessary to work overtime or take a second job to reduce his debt."

That's what America has been doing since the crisis hit in 2008. "...the Keynesians are still surprised and annoyed that the economy has not recovered. Their answer is to spend more, borrow more, and increase the debt even faster. It's hard to believe that reasonable people believe this. An individual is not better off by assuming more debt and spending more, so how can a nation expect to be?"

Keynesians in Washington:

Demagogue the issue with innuendos and false charges regarding compassion.

Call anyone who opposes unlimited unemployment benefits heartless.

"The question they won't even consider is what would they do if it were shown that extracting funds from the productive economy to subsidize unemployment prolongs the unemployment and actually increases the number of jobs lost? If a reversal of this process is not achieved, total bankruptcy will force us to consider an entirely new system."

Congressman Paul believes we need another currency based on human choice. "That would require an end of a crackdown on competitive currencies. I am fully confident that we would see a dollar out-competed in time."

Editor's Note: have studied the works of Bill Still and am convinced that the answer to America's monetary problems is to end the Fed and print our own non-interest-bearing, debt-free green backs as Lincoln did to finance the Civil War. It would take us out of the money crisis that threatens to put us into a deep depression and would solve all of our money problems. Because the answer is quite evident, I am somewhat surprised that Dr. Paul didn't even mentioned this solution to our problems in this chapter. Read on. Maybe he will later on.

Hayek, F.A. 2009, in Currency A Way To Stop Inflation. Auburn, AL: Mises Institute.

Paul, Ron. [1982] 2008, Case For Gold, Auburn, AL, Mises Institute.

Rothbard, Murray. [1963] 2008. Has Government Done To Our Money? Auburn, AL. Mises Institute.

Editor's note: a related matter, we are seeing the negative results of government trying to spend its way out of a problem in the Federal Housing Administration. As of December, 2011, it is in violation of the two percent capital reserve ratio law because they hold dramatically few reserves for their trillion dollars in loans. If you are going to grow your way out of a deep hole, as Secretary Donavon says he is, you do not make risky loans as he has done to many people with such low FICA credit scores. This agency now insures more than one-third of all mortgages in the United States. Thus, this type of government meddling in the housing market is surely going to result in a huge bailout, again hitting taxpayers hard. This, despite the progress that Secretary Donavon claims he has made

31

Moral Hazard

Lack of Morals In America

Causes Serious Consequences

Our society is engulfed in moral hazard that results in serious unintended economic consequences. Let me explain moral hazard from an insurance standpoint. Insurers go out of their way not to insure "moral hazards," that is a house that is already on fire, a community already confronted with a known tornado or hurricane already a few miles out of town. It would be morally wrong for the insurance carrier's underwriters to accept these kinds of clear and present risks—losses from such risks that are already occurring. No insurance company will do that.

But the federal government takes on moral risk, especially when you get a majority of progressives passing bills. It is because they view government belonging to the minority who, for example, are unemployed or don't have enough money to make their mortgage payment or pay for their tuition loans. Progressive government sees this as an opportunity to gain personal political advantage and stand out in the eyes of the poor. Their maxim is, "Provide housing or some other benefit for the poor and you gain a voter for life."

Well, that is exactly what Barney Frank, Chris Dodd, and Chuck Schumer did in the Congress. They were slick talkers who not only convinced other members of Congress and President George Bush that it was a good idea to make sure everyone—even those who couldn't afford one—got a house and that their loan applications were approved by the banks.

What a miserable mistake that was! Free and easy loaning habits of progressive permeated the banking industry all the way from the local bank that knew it didn't have to underwrite loans because it could sell all of them to the FHA or to Fannie Mae or Freddie Mac who went out of business until Barak Obama made a very unintelligent decision to revive them with government money, effectively making them government agencies. Essentially, that is what caused the housing bubble of 2008 that led to the financial crisis and the jobs debacle that we find ourselves in today—one that progressives are trying to lie their way out of by manipulating job numbers.

In December, 2008 the government announced the jobless rate had dramatically for no apparent reason—dropped from 9 percent to 8.6 percent. That surprising revelation came just two days after the Department of Labor Statistics announced that the number of people seeking welfare (jobless benefits) spiked again to over 400,000 for the month of October, 2011. Well, here's how it happened. Some 316,000 people in December got discouraged because they couldn't find a job and took themselves off the jobless roles. The Obama government saw them coming and purposely called them employed, which wasn't true. This bumped up the number of employed in December, despite the fact that nothing good had happened in jobs.

We don't have more jobs, we just have a creatively liberal government department. All of these Obama appointees represent moral hazards. Dishonesty in office is rampant.

Important Facts:

The past 50 years has given us an epidemic of government intrusions in all economic decisions.

<u>The results have been an exponential growth of consequences that represent moral hazard.</u>

All government policies have resulted in unintended consequences.

Government promises our people will be protected from every conceivable risk.

These include natural disasters, health problems, and economic needs to foreign threats.

The government is now expected to protect us from ourselves, from all of our unwise behavior.

Government protecting people from themselves should be offensive to anyone who loves liberty: Progressives promise that government will ensure that everything we use or take into our bodies is safe and beneficial.

If we need an immunization, no need to think. The government will pay and provide for it.

No personal responsibility is required in making decisions.

No market-directed consumer groups seem able to supersede D.C.'s bureaucratic decisions involving everyone.

When mistakes are made with central economic planning, the consequences are horrendous and magnified.

Unfortunately, non-suspecting, non-thinking people accept government lies that we will be taken care of without lost freedoms.

Ron Paul believes the above are reasons we are facing an economic and political crisis today.

Moral hazard does involve immoral behavior, contrary to popular belief.

Congressman Paul uses a broad definition for "moral hazard." It includes government policies, assurances, insurance, myths, guarantees, clichés, false notions, lies, emotional arguments and economic planning.

It also has to do with policies adopted in foreign affairs as well as to regulate personal habits.

"Most of our national government actions are hazardous to morality. Government assumption of illicit power starts the process, and it spreads to the special interests which use these powers to serve their own interest. Though they may do this consciously for gain, the ultimate hazard later on cancels out the benefits they may have gained."

Home building and mortgage credit benefit from easy credit in the short run.

But later on there are bad consequences beyond government expectation..

The government acts immorally by illegally assuming it powers.

The business interests yield to the offer and act immorally by participating in the political process.

The Financial Crisis Inquiry Commission established by Congress established a group called Percora Investigation. It was charged with determining cause and effect. Paul said it isn't any more successful this time than during its inquiry of 1932. Why? Because it is largely influenced by progressive economists.

Congressman Paul said they were totally oblivious to free market Austrian economics. They had no understanding about how artificially low interest rates and Federal Reserve policy are the culprits. It's a cover-up. Their policies created a problem they can't fix because they can't properly diagnose it.

They blame free markets, sound money, and lack of regulation for the crisis.

Paul has no faith in government commissions to objectively sort out the issues. These guys didn't even recognize a problem brewing soon enough to do anything positive. Paul said this of the progressives:

One group steals, one becomes the "fence," and the recipient (the public) doesn't complain until the "magic" wears off and the economic system unravels. But only the well established are given bailouts. Justifying moral hazard "as a benign economic reaction should be seen as part of the grand scheme of central economic planning." That includes regulating personal habits and enforcing foreign policy and the harm that results. planners—in a patented knee jerk reaction—order up more regulation and promises to solve the problems. It doesn't work and the problems start all over again.

32

Morality In Government

In brief, here's a partial reason

for our current economic crisis:

The government operates without a moral compass. The rule of law is meaningless. There is little respect for principles of liberty. Neo-cons—people like Mitt Romney, Rick Santorum, and Newt Gingrich—follow modern liberals and people like Leo Strauss and Irving Kristol. They accept the principle of authoritarianism and provide little or no moral leadership. Unfortunately, most Americans expect to be taken care of by government. Where the resources will come from is not known. The hard work ethic has become passé to many Americans.

Many Americans show little concern about the morality of a welfare state and massive economic intervention. Ron Paul says that those on the receiving end of the government transfer system—poor, middle class, and wealthy alike—refuse to be concerned about whether the whole system is based on a moral principle. He says it would never occur to them that theft and violence is used to carry out these principles.

It seems to this author that our drift from religious principles has led to this decay of our moral principles. Paul blames the transition away from the original reasons for our country's founding. Government was to be strictly limited. Its purpose was to protect the borders, but also to protect us from an authoritarian government. This drift away from original purposes for our country's founding has been going on for a long time.

In early March, 2012, Conservative radio commentator Rush Limbaugh decried the recent invitation of a liberal student (age 30) to a Congressional hearing for the express purpose of hitting up members for public money to have sex. While the girl, a law school student, didn't use exactly those terms, the meaning was that someone—taxpayers like you and I—other than those having sex should pay for the condoms. The Democratic subcommittee "hearing" was sponsored and the invitation given by the Democratic leader in the House, Nancy Pelosi, to a 30-year-old Georgetown coed who does not belong to the Catholic Church. This is a Jesuit Catholic school.

She intimated that it is government's obligation, not hers, to provide to her and her fellow female students "free" condoms because to refuse to do so could cause an epidemic among school kids wanting sex one to three times a day. She said refusal to help her in this way would put law students further into debt and she wanted a total of $3,000 from the taxpayers for each of those females which would last them, at a buck a condom, three years while in law school. For some reason progressives today do not believe it is stealing from the taxpayers when they are called upon to pay for such personal things.

One thing usually leads to another. Can you imagine the uproar among all female students in America if we paid for one school's condoms and not for every girl's condoms in the nation? And what about white collar and blue collar workers? They could rise up and prove discrimination. It would probably not end until we had to pay for all female condoms out of the federal budget, including those used by Nancy Pelosi and other lawmakers themselves. Yes, I can see why Nancy

Pelosi is for this. She is a progressive bent on turning up-side-down the nation's mores, laws, institutions and traditional religious values such as that of marriage being a union between one man and one woman, values of which as each day passes Pelosi proves more and more that she has less and less.

It is hard to justify any of this. But one can see how the morals of Americans have deteriorated. It is not as John F. Kennedy said, "Ask not what my government can do for me, but what can I do for my country?"

No, Limbaugh was not wrong in ripping into this shameless young woman. He may also be correct to assume she was a "plant" by Barak Obama and his cohorts to create controversy among conservative presidential candidates over women. At that time Democrats were broadcasting the idea that Republicans do not like women, and it all stems from the fact that Barak Obama's re-election poll numbers were way down in the female category. With this president, everything is politics—everything is a ruse.

He missed the point. A new survey out in March, 2012 from the National Marriage Project shows that marriage is an institution in

decline in many parts of American society. This "retreat from marriage in Middle America" will have wide-ranging social, economic, and spiritual consequences. One recent important study about marriage that I wanted to talk about administered by the Pew Research Center, showed that nearly 40% of Americans believe marriage is becoming obsolete. Another study shows that today more babies are born to unmarried womenage 30 and under, 51 percent, than to married women.

*The brazen-faced Georgetown student "plant" who visited a Congressional subcommittee to ask for aid for all students at her school for the purchase of condomns is typical of students from liberal families today. While Rush Limbau*gh may have called her a slut and other names for asking for public money to carry on her sexual activities, when President Barak Obama weighed in it became a news story unworthy of national attention, showing which party it is that wants people to be self reliant and to live according to our founders' principles of limited government and which political party always insists on government (taxpayers) paying for personal things that it rightly should keep its nose out of.

A few years ago, even democratic congressmen and women had the good sense to leave sex out of politics, but since abortion is such a big issue in this year's (2012) presidential elections, the president—at all times and on occasions a political animal—needed to show the students on which side of the fence he resided. Was there ever any doubt? He is a big-government advocate and a big spender, and anything goes as long as he can do it with someone else's money. With this president, everything is to garner more votes for his re-election so that he can add to the national debt and destroy the Constitution little by little.

Unfortunately, Washington responds to voter "noise" for ultimate security and an economic safety net.

These people's voices seem to drown out those of us who ask only for liberty.

The time when government was held in check by constitutional limitations has been long forgotten.

Paul believes that even the Constitution itself weakened this principle that was embedded in Articles of Confederation. In this he is like the great States rights patriot Patrick Henry.

It wasn't until the Twentieth Century that the moral compass guarding our liberties was completely cast aside.

Congressman Paul asks, "What moral system should government follow?" He answers, "The same one individuals follow.

1. Do not steal

2. Do not murder

3. Do not bear false witness

4. Do not covet

5. Do not foster vice

I really relate to his final conclusion: "If governments would merely follow the moral law that all religions recognize, we would live in a world of peace, prosperity, and freedom. The system is called classical liberalism. Liberty is not complicated." (Classical Liberalism is an old term meaning true conservatism).

33

Noble Lie

Can "Good" Come From A Lie?

Plato argued that benefits from the Noble Lie are a moral good. In the late twentieth century it had been argued that modern-day rulers had license to lie because of their natural intellectual superiority.

Ron Paul calls neoconservatives present-day champions of the noble lie, and their influence is strongly bipartisan. (Neo-cons among the GOP include both Bushes, Mitt Romney, Rick Santorum, and Newt Gingrich.) The word literally means "new conservative." They champion pre-emptive wars, and a little lying is okay as long as it is motivated by what they call "the greater good."

Leo Strauss is the modern-day mentor of neoconservatives. His mentors? Plato and Machiavelli. The principle of lying and deception for the people's benefit is endorsed by each administration regardless of party.

Lying is reserved for the nobility. It is not for the common person who might lie on his IRS form and get thrown in jail. Lying is reserved for the powerful and those who claim they are the only ones who can take care of the ignorant and disillusioned masses.

Here are Ron Paul's words: "In Mein Kampf Kamlph, Hitler argued that if governments made their lies colossal, nobody would challenge the notion that anybody could deliberately make up something so far from the truth." Read what Hitler's first lieutenant in crime, Hermann Goering, had to say in 1946 from his Nuremberg prison cell. This was from G.M. Gilbert's Diary:

Why would some poor man on a farm want to risk his life in a war when the best that he can get out of it is to come back in one piece? But, after all, it's the leaders of the country who determine the policy and it's a simple matter to drag the people along, whether it is a democracy or a fascist dictatorship or a communist dictatorship. That is easy…all you have to do is tell them you are being attacked and denounce the pacifist for lack of patriotism and exposing the country to danger. It works the same way in any country.

This may not seem astounding to those who have studied the two Bush administrations. Leo Strauss came to the United States in 1938 at the age of thirty-nine and built a reputation at the University of Chicago, where he influenced a lot of future administrators and appointees of the George W. Bush administration.

People who influenced our foreign policy over the past decade:

1. Paul Wolfowitz

2. Abram Shulsky

3. William Kristol

4. Irving Kristol

5. John Podhorerz

6. Michael Ledeen

7. Stephen Cambone

8. Richard Perle

The Ideas of Strauss are quite frightening:

*They lead to political instability and immorality.

*Views are based on rejection of trust in a free society

*Unless refuted, only tyranny can result

Here are some of the Neo-cons' erroneous ideas:

*The elite have a responsibility to deceive the masses

*Rulers are superior and must rule over inferior people

*A compliant society responds positively to a cynical use of religion. This prevents individuals from independent thinking

*External threats unite the people; If a threat doesn╤ft exist, leaders must create one

*Threats unite people and they become more obedient to the state

*Manycons believe individualism is basically evil and the elite must meet their obligations to rule the incompetent

*To suppress individualism and fortify the ruling elite, religion, lies, and war are needed

Because leaders from all parties agree with the above, neo-cons can suppress individualism and fortify a ruling elite. This is why individualism is under constant attack and the philosophy of the American Founders has been so severely undermined. Neo-cons would "blow their cover" if they did not deny they believed in these principles.

Neo-cons do the opposite, claiming title to super-patriotism and anyone who disagrees with their wars and welfare schemes is un-American, unpatriotic, not humanitarian, and against the troops.

Neo-conservatives dread the day the people demand to hear the truth. "War propaganda is a well-known phenomenon and even though many are aware of it, its incessant use by government officials and media works rather well in pushing people into a pro-war frenzy."

This is the very reason Congressman Paul refuses to attend the top-secret briefings for updates on a current crisis. He knows they will be filled with propaganda and spin for political cover.

Important revelations about the workings of government invariable do not come from the liberal major network media, but from independent networks. (Rush Limbaugh's EIB Network, for example.) These people are willing to take the risks and fallout if they are wrong. The drive-by media isn't.

Progressives think in weird ways. For example, Irving Kristol argued that there should be different sets of truth for different categories of people. The religious idea that one set of truths should apply to all has been overthrown by these elites.

Communism says that only the party, not religion, can set the truth, and it was not rigid. It changed according to circumstances and political priorities. Peace, progress, and prosperity are impossible under these circumstances.

34

Patriotism

Don White Meets A Muslim From

Morocco At The Car Dealership

I enjoyed myself while waiting for my old car to have new back brakes installed. It's a gas guzzler that we use rarely but when I do, I love the car. I walked over to the showroom and sat in one of the new cars. Up came a swarthy good-looking young car salesman about age 35 from Morocco, North Africa. He said he had been in the states for 13 years but had yet to become a citizen. I encouraged him to take out citizenship and he demurred. I said to myself, here is a dedicated illegal alien.

We carried on a lively conversation. He was very patriotic to his religion, Islam, as I am to mine,

Church of Jesus Christ of Latter-day Saints. He said Morocco would never riot as they did in Egypt and Libya because they love their ruler, King Mohammad The Sixth. This ruler changes things according to the desires of the people and is not a tyrant. He said many people living now in Israel comprising a lot of the population of Israel had been Jews living in Morocco in 1948 when the UN, with U.S. support, made Israel an independent nation. He conceded that Moroccans like the Jews, but not necessarily their government.

I'm not sure what his feelings were for the United States. I assume he likes it here better than his home country, though I'm sure in the back of his head is the idea that our American presidents (Bush and Obama) have done a lot of collateral damage to life, limb, and property while carrying on their wars in the Middle East. I am against these unnecessary wars and that's not unpatriotic, and I'll tell you why.

Our military generals and the elites in the U.S. have patriotism backwards. **Many wrongly believe you're not patriotic if:**

You don't support funding for illegal, undeclared wars

You don't support a flag-burning amendment

You dare to challenge the powers of the state.

"Patriotism never demands obedience to the state, but rather obedience to the principles of liberty," said Ron Paul.

Paul believes there is a vast difference between supporting the "government" than supporting the people. "You must support the people," he believes, "even under threat of government punishment."

Samuel Johnson in 1775 said: "Patriotism is the lost refuge of the scoundrel."

Paul elucidates that by saying: "There are quite a few of those [scoundrels] in Washington. The arrogance and manipulation of passing a piece of legislation that severely undermines the Fourth Amendment and calling it the Patriot Act says it all." This is false patriotism.

"Few politicians once in office remain faithful to their patriotic ideas. "The aphrodisiac of power overwhelms individuals who go into government with high ideals. Championing change as an outsider is easily morphed into patriotic fervor to protest the state once the politicians become part of what they previously agreed was the enemy."

It's a powerful argument for not giving power to elected or unelected officials, since so few remain diligent defenders of individual rights. "Loyalty to bad policy for patriotic reasons, no matter how harmful it's been on us, is always folly. Patriotism always demands victory and success no matter how foolish and harmful. No one is permited to acknowledge a mistake in policy. Bad policies are continued for "patriotic" reasons, even when seeking a victory or success tha's elusive."

The kind of patriotism our neoconservatives and progressives have "evokes a support comparable to the divine right of kings." It used to be heresy to challenge the church. Today's heresy is to challenge the state because it demands a true change in policy and by doing so admits to our egregious past errors. Changing of disloyalty and lack of patriotism are loudly heard. Paul believes that today's heresy is to challenge the state, "something not tolerated by the elites in charge of our government."

True patriots should demand that government not act in secrecy

Government transparency is the credo of a patriot

Loyalty to the people should not be confused with loyalty to the government

If one is forced to choose between the two, it is evident that government has excessive power.

When the two are in opposition, it is the duty of the patriot to work for the people even if doing so requires opposition to the government

Some say that blind "patriotism" to government is always required of a patriot. If that were so, America would still be a colony of Great Britain and subjects of the King of England.

If that were so, America would still be a colony of England and subjects of the King of England. Paul believes "it is better said that a patriot's responsibility is to condemn the evil actions of government rather than endearing them by either supporting them or ignoring them in the name of patriotism."

Failing to admit the errors of their ways has caused our leaders to be responsible for countless American casualties and deaths. This has caused the noble warrior image. It plagued both Lyndon Johnson and Richard Nixon. "Look how long [they] refused to admit the truth, even at a cost of tens of thousands of American and Vietnamese casualties."

Congressman Paul said, "Even today, walking away from a useless and stupid, senseless war in Central Asia is impossible because the American majority are still—in spite of recent and ancient history—demanding a macho victory regardless of cost and with nothing to be gained and lives to be lost."

"The glory of victory in senseless war should never replace the dignity of peace in a sane world."

35

Political Correctness

Is Our Obsession With Political

Correctness An Epidemic?

Ron Paul and millions of other Americans believe that our obsession with political correctness (PC) is epidemic.

Some people lose their jobs over PC, while others are immune from criticism. Candidates have had to quit running for office over what the media believes they did wrong.

Politicians mock their opponents for what they regard is the incorrect use of words, and the liberal media are quick to join in the condemnation.

Those who play the game of political correctness do it for various reasons:

Control and power over others

Promoting a political agenda

Scoring political points

An attempt to show that challengers to politically incorrect speech are morally superior

More often they are driven by a feeling of inferiority

An attempt to prove themselves with the pretense of moral courage

There are now many words we cannot say because political correctness forbids it:

Racist comments

Sexist words

Homophobic language

People who want these words and phrases to disappear have to be insecure and easily intimidated. Paul believes that when the draft appears necessary again, women, lesbians, and gay people will be drafted along with heterosexual men to fight our wars. Paul says the "silliness has made fools of those who get carried away with enforcing the extremes."

The results of equal rights feminist movements were not all beneficial. "Sometimes it meant that women would be subject to grueling conditions just as happened to men—like being placed in harms way in no-win undeclared wars."

He believes that if there were no plans to draft men as well as women some time in the future, draft registration would have been eliminated some time ago.

"Women will demand inclusiveness, yet when offensive language or jokes are told they will run to authorities complaining that they are offended and that guilty parties must be reprimanded or punished." Paul believes this whole idea of political and social correctness can get worse. "Already there have been attempts at banning books and songs with words deemed offensive to particular groups. He believes it won't take much for political correctness advocates to target the correctness of political views and ideas.

All totalitarian societies seek to control thoughts and ideas. "I have been excluded from certain political events," said Paul, "because of my "controversial" political views."

Ron Paul said, "We already have laws on the books that require lesser penalties for those who commit crimes against 'straight' people because these crimes were not motivated by politically incorrect thinking."

The hate police, or the thought police, are entrenched in our legislative and judicial process, and political correctness. Though at times it seems silly and frivolous, they might well "evolve into a federal police effort to maintain order when society becomes unruly in difficult economic times. Maintaining order and safety is the goal at all costs in a totalitarian system. Under those conditions, liberty becomes the enemy."

36

Prohibition

Prohibition Is Not Compatible

With A Free Society

Dr. Paul is against government manipulation in the use of certain substances:

Food, Drugs, Alcohol

Ron Paul calls these intrusions dangerous. "Prohibition is motivated by busybodies who have a gross misunderstanding of the unintended consequences of attempts to improve other people's habits and consumption through government force. Time and time again we are shown that it simply does not work."

The congressman states that if there are to be any regulations on certain substances...this should be done by the individual states, not by the federal government.

On January 29, 1919 Congress passed the 18th Amendment. This alcohol prohibition bill was motivated by a desire to stop drunkenness and the consequences of excessive drinking. Paul claims that those who pushed for this bill did so without concern for the large majority of drinkers who drank responsibly, or that it would violate their constitutional rights.

Many were required to give up their freedom of choice in order to stop the excesses of a few. Paul praises Franklin D. Roosevelt who "ushered in the repeal of prohibition. This made the country freer and won for FDR the affection of millions of Americans.

Prohibition brought in the era of backyard stills, and bootlegging, leading to blindness and death. Paul said that many lost their lives in the violence that occurred over prohibition, just as is happening today over illegal drugs.

America has had millions of accidents and thousands of drunk driving deaths that concern all of us. But it has also had its share of disease and addiction which is a personal matter, not that of the government or the taxpayers. People are responsible for their own actions. When will liberal America learn that?

Progressives believe just the opposite. Since someone must pay for the medical bills of people who abuse drugs or alcohol, they see it their opportunity to expand government by filling the void with another federal mandate and handout of taxpayer money. From this, Paul takes it one step further. He posits that local and national governments will dictate our eating, smoking, drinking, and exercise habits to keep healthcare costs down.

The result will be a loss of liberty. From this, we expect the government to give us good health? "Hardly," shouts Ron Paul. It never works out that way.

Paul has studied the issue and comes up with the only logical answer. We must legalize drugs in America and away goes the problem. That may never happen because lawmakers are too interested in preserving their positions in Congress.

"My position on the drug war has been known for years, and in spite of any opponents using it against me, it has seemingly never hurt me in my reelection efforts. And my district is a Bible Belt conservative district."

Ron Paul believes the people are a lot more sophisticated about the issue than the politicians give them credit. It has been far more expensive to fight the drug wars than it was to fight crime associated with prohibition.

His guess is that someday the people will wake up and decide, as we did in 1933, that prohibition to improve personal behavior is a lost cause. Dr. Paul believes the states must reassert themselves to provide more responsible governance than we now have from the federal level.

"The federal government is inept. The Tenth Amendment is about to be reborn." Powers not delegated by the states to the federal government are reserved to the states or to the people.

There is reliable evidence that drug laws have done nothing to reduce drug usage while contributing significantly to street crime. "Freedom of choice for one's actions solves a lot of dilemmas when it comes to the proper role of government in our lives."

37

Public Land

Ownership of Land In America

This chapter should be rightly called "Argument For Private Land."

Briefly, here is the problem:

>One third of he land in America is federally owned.

>Federal ownership of land east of the Mississippi is minimal.

>Federal ownership of land west of the Mississippi is massive.

>In the west, the feds have held onto vast acreages of land.

>Federal management of land is atrocious.

>It is bureaucratic and inefficient, serving special interests.

>Interior Department land management is poor.

Management of federal land is mainly picking beneficiaries of public land or prohibiting any development. Rarely is it to turn the land over to the states for the purpose of being sold. Why do we need the feds to manage western lands and stifle progress? Taxation and regulation are so cumbersome that "landowners" are essentially renters with no rights to the land.

When you have a third of the land in America federally owned, especially in the west this smacks of communism. Those lands must be given out to ordinary citizens either to homestead or to purchase.

School taxes are especially onerous and create a problem for the western states and some in the east that cannot tax federal lands. Nor can they tax Indian lands, though they must provide special services and infrastructure.

The answer? Turn these lands over to the states.

Regulation governing land use, from states to the federal government, "makes developing the land horribly difficult

To make changes on the land, the "renter" must get approval from all entities surrounding the land: cities, counties, and states.

Each jurisdiction has many overlapping regulations

Often, radical environmentalists hold up or prevent land use

Who are the seemingly noxious entities wielding power over your use of public lands?

- The Environmental Protection Agency

  Fish and Wildlife

- The Department of Homeland Security

- Federal Emergency Management Agency

- The Corps of Engineers

Many people believe that extra land is needed for future or current national parks. Therefore, they don't question the government for holding such large parcels of land from private people and entities and ruling it with a tight fist. The truth is that most public lands are not part of a public park and never will be used that way.

It is very expensive to hold parks open to the ublic. It requires public expenditures for roads, bridges, walking paths, signs, restrooms, and gathering places and other facilities. It requires National Park personnel to man the parks almost twelve months of the year.

Ron Paul conjectures that in a free society, which America is not, private entities such as Ducks Unlimited or The Nature Conservancy may be the types of organizations that would provide national parks.

How Should We Pay For Parks

- Maintenance fees for all?

- Users fees?

- Tax all people, including 90 percent or more who don't use the parks?

There are rich people who manage to purchase a parcel of land in a national forest, for example, build a home or a cabin and arrange to see to it that the park never sells land to anyone else and that all services to and around their land are paid for by society at large. This is both unfair and shortsighted land use.

Paul said Texas is a good example of how private ownership of land facilitated proper use of natural resources—"especially oil, gas, and coal. "Over time," Paul said, "for economic reasons, land was broken up into smaller and smaller pieces. Ownership of the oil was divided according to private property rights, which allowed many less wealthy people to benefit."

The Congressman said that the entrepreneurs took the risks and the benefits were spread generously to the workers who labored in the industry. He believes joining the Union was probably a mistake for Texas. Before that time, the Republic of Texas owned very little land. Paul contends that "Texas never needed the federal government to manage its progress, whether it concerned natural resources, agriculture, or ranching."

The Federal government should turn over its land to the states to be sold. The natural monument issues would present the greatest resistance. By making this an exception, "a lot could be accomplished by turning millions of acres over to the states. As the lands are sold, a portion of the funds could be used to lower the national debt."

This move toward privatizing public lands hasn't yet caught the imagination of other lawmakers. It may have to be reserved for a time when the federal government isn't bankrupt like it is today. God help us get over our time bomb problems, and if bankruptcy is what is needed to make Americans understand and prod people into action, let it come sooner rather than later. But the truth is this: The government should want to divest itself of large capital outlays associated with the Interior Department management of federal lands. I know they would if Ron Paul were president.

Using eminent domain to increase the size of government land holdings

"The Fifth Amendment was written more to assure that land taken by the government was adequately paid for than to give the right to government to confiscate property at will."

Three reasons given for use of eminent domain:

Road easements

Utility easements

Parks

Paul said that recently public domain has become an instrument to serve special interests. "The Fifth Amendment was written assuming the government would take property only for public use—never for someone else's private benefit. Corporations have hijacked local government by lying to them. The promise is that eminent domain land taken by the company will cause surrounding land values to rise. That should mean that businesses will pay more taxes, the municipality will benefit, and the new (eminent domain) business will earn more money with its new, preferable location.

Sounds like a good deal, the Congressman said, except for the individual who was forced to sell the land and lose his or her rights of property ownership. This is a modern distortion and abuse of the principle of eminent domain. But Ron Paul believes that we should be headed in the opposite direction that makes it more difficult to force eminent domain on anyone. We should not be allowing it for the benefit of some special interest.

We have strayed from the truth. Many, even in government, lack a clear understanding of the right to own private property. This is ...crucial in maintaining a free society. Without this, a free society cannot exist.

38

Racism

Ron Paul defines racism as:

The defining and disparaging of a whole people due primarily to its racial, ethnic, or religious makeup which leads to the desire to deny an individual or group full rights in the civic community, and the related impulse to see some harm come to an individual or group through private or public means.

It's a crass and cruel denial of individualism. Congressman Paul says that a racist believes that some group trait always trumps all individual traits. It's like a white person who sees no good in any action or words of a black person; or a black economist who disagrees with the socialist bias of the NAACP. In the latter case, the economist's thoughts may be dismissed with the comment, "He's not thinking like a black."

Based on group prejudice, blacks can disparage whites and vice versa. "During the great wave of European immigration to the United States in the late nineteenth century," said Paul, "the anti-Italian and anti-Irish feelings on the part of the majority might have been understandable from historical context, but they led to real effects in the form of political disabilities being imposed on these groups."

He said it was the same with the Jim Crow laws that followed Reconstruction in the South. "Such laws not only violated human rights they led to long-simmering resentments that had terrible human and political consequences."

During the First and Second World Wars, German people were conscientiously denigrated by government propaganda efforts. During War II, the Japanese were not only discriminated against with words and salacious posters, tens of thousands of Japanese (110,000, to be more accurate) were interned in government War Relocation Camps (concentration camps). This was not only a violation of human rights, it led to long-simmering resentments that Paul says "had terrible human and political consequences."

During the Cold War, Russians were suspected of being communists until they openly proclaimed their hatred for the rules of their homeland. Today, post 9/11, many Americans are suspicious of Arab nationals living in the United States. Christians are being told that we have always been at war with Muslims, that they are a war-like people. That they are taking over America with their mosques, clothing, and Sharia law.

Paul says "this whole campaign has the earmarks of a new Cold War, and perhaps hot war, in which Islam replaces atheistic communism as the enemy of choice." Paul believes it has nothing to do with reality. "The 9/11 Muslim hijackers were not devout Muslims, but we are often led to believe they were." Government propagandists want us to believe that the struggle with Islam is our most important foreign policy priority.

"Peace can happen again," said Paul, "but only if the United States stops occupying Arab countries. I really do not know what is worse: the false claims of racism or the harboring of prejudice.   An example is the actual sponsorship of racism by the government itself in wartime, support of affirmative action, and quotas in the name of ending racism. All of these actions are contrary to the individualism that a free society should uphold without regard to race."

39

Religion And Liberty

Wars of Religion

Congressman Paul begins this chapter by suggesting that there are many distorted views of war, depending on whether you are an atheist or a member of a religion. While it is true, history bears out the fact that certain religious leaders did lead their people into wars where people were killed, secular killing far outstrips those killed in religious aggression or defense of land. "Estimates are that the godless dictators of these nations [fascist and communist atheists] killed 262 million of their own people, far surpassing the estimated 44 million military personnel killed in war.

He says when one looks at religious wars, he comes away with a distorted understanding of religious beliefs. Within all major religions, he says, there are extremists who promote violence in the name of God. I assume he hasn't studied very many

American religions—people such as the Latter-day Saints, Amish, Baptists, and others who have not displayed tendencies toward war. But then, he was only referring to the world's largest religions, wasn't he?

When religions killed and made war, they did so—one presumes—by distorting the religion and following a false doctrine. "It should not be assumed that it was that religion itself that prompted the violence. Instead of religious beliefs being the cause of war, it is more likely that those who want war co-opt religion and falsely claim the enemy is attacking their religious values."

Paul asks an interesting question: How often have we heard neoconservatives repeat the mantra that religious fanatics attack us for our freedoms and prosperity? "Neoconservatives deliberately use religion to stir up hatred toward the enemy."

He explains where the Arab Taliban came from. The Soviet occupation spurred the growth of the religion-driven Mujahedeen which later was called the Taliban. That the United States actively financed and encouraged the teaching of radical Islam to fight the Soviets is no secret. "What we didn't understand," says Paul, "is that the radicalization of religious beliefs would someday be directed against us—as it was on 9/11.

Congressman Paul is right: Islam does not teach that the mass killing of innocent individuals is moral. "Yet foreign occupation can serve as a tremendous incentive to radicalize religious beliefs."

And Ron Paul is so right again when he says " Christian imperialism that endorses preventive war in the Middle East should not be allowed to destroy the message delivered by the Prince of Peace." It's a great distortion to use Christianity in any way to justify aggression and violence.

"The Christian message is that no tyrant can destroy the dignity and self-worth of any individual, regardless of circumstances."

Obviously, this man Ron Paul understands the Savior's role very well. He said "Christ deals with spiritual matters, not temporal or political. "Salvation for believers was the message, not drawing future geographic boundaries in a small portion of the world."

Force should never be used to impose one people's views on another. "The Founders were right to reject the notion that the federal government be permitted to establish an official religion without being hostile to those who express their spiritual views in private or public places."

A free society protects the rights of both those espousing atheist and religious beliefs. The principle of the Golden Rule has been sanctioned by all great religions. When violence has been used by great religions, it has been done without theological justification. Then Mr. Paul gives us a list that was developed by the site RaceMatters.org.

LOVE IN GREAT RELIGIONS

Christianity: "Beloved, let us love one another, for love is of God; and everyone that loveth is born of God, and knoweth God. He that loveth not, knoweth not God, for God is Love."

Confucianism: "To love all men is the greatest benevolence."

Buddhism: "Let a man cultivate towards the whole world a heart of love."

Hinduism: "One can best worship the Lord through love."

Islam: "Love is this, that thou shouldst account thyself very little and God very great."

Sikhism: "God will regenerate those in whose hearts there is love."

Judaism: "Thou shalt love the Lord thy God with all thy heart, and thy neighbor as thyself."

Jainism: "The days are of most profit to him who acts in love."

Zoroastrianism: Man is the beloved of the Lord, and should love him in return.

Baha: "Love me that I may love thee. If thou lovest Me not, My love can no wise reach thee."

Shinto: "Love is the representative of the Lord."

GOLDEN RULE…And the World's Great Religions

Christianity: "All things whatsoever ye would that men should do to you, do ye even so to them." (Matthew 7:12)

Confucianism: "Do not unto others what you would not have them do unto you."

Buddhism: "Hurt not others in ways that you yourself would find hurtful." (Udana-Varga. 5:18)

Baha: "Blessed is he who preferred his brother before himself." (Baha'u'llah, , 71)

Islam: "Hurt no one that no one may hurt you." (Muhammad, "The Farewell Sermon.")

Judaism: "That which is hateful to you do not do to your fellow."

Humanists and Atheists do not condemn the Golden Rule.

PEACE AND GREAT RELIGIONS

Christianity: Blessed are the peacemakers, for they shall be called the children of   God.

Judaism: "When a man's ways please the Lord, he maketh even his enemies to be   at peace with him.

Buddhism: There is no happiness greater than peace.

Hinduism: Without meditation, where is peace? Without peace where is happiness?

Islam: God will guide men to peace. If they will heed him. He will lead them   from   the darkness of war to the light of peace.

Shinto: Let the Earth be free from trouble and men live at peace under the   protection of the Divine.

Baha: War is death while peace is life.

Sikhism: Only in the Name of the Lord do we find our peace.

Confucianism: Seek to be in harmony with all your neighbors …live in peace with your brethren.

Mahatma Gandhi: "Like the bee gathering honey from different flowers, the wise   person accepts the essence of different scriptures and sees only   the good in all religions."

THE TEN COMMANDMENTS

The Ten Commandments are traditionally known to be part of the foundation of Christianity and Judaism. The Qur'an in different places essentially repeats the Ten Commandments, indicating that Muslims do not believe that this message has been corrupted from their divine origin as other provisions of the Torah and the Gospels allegedly have.

The Qur'an endorses One God; No idol worship; Do not take God's name in vain; One day a week for special prayers; Honor our parents; Do not murder; Do not commit adultery; Do not steal; Do not withhold testimony; Do not covet what others have.

RON PAUL'S CONCLUSION:

"These great religions represent billions of people who agree on love, the Golden Rule, and the Ten Commandments. We are brought together by believing in one God, supposedly the same one, yet we fight and hate and lack tolerance and understanding. The positive truth is perverted and replaced by arrogant enforcers willing to initiate war and aggression for selfish interests while distorting religious belief."

The contemptable neo-conservatives are modern Machiavellians. It is true: Some of them even admit they diligently use extreme religious beliefs not to promote love and peace, but to galvanize people to fight and supposedly to preserve the true religion, "It is this influence by antireligious non-believers that incites hatred between the different religions and that leads to so much violence and hatred. A better understanding and greater tolerance would provide the courage for believers of different faiths to resist the political demagogues who for their own selfish reasons use violence as the tool for managing their tyrannical governments.

HOW NEO-CONS USE WAR

To justify geopolitical goals

To gain control over the world's oil supplie

HOW MUSLIMS VIEW WAR

Bad foreign policy

Radical religious views in the West

Bad foreign and domestic policy invites extremism in religious activities—on both sides, according to Ron Paul. Though most religions and most people accept the Golden rule, some could care less. "There are those who have no self-esteem and are self-haters and naturally self-destructive. Why would they care about treating others better than they treat themselves when they don't place any value on their own lives? Put a person like this in charge of other people and trouble results. It's not too infrequent that individuals like this find a way to the top of the political heap. Being insecure and hateful, participating in violence to bring about good things to compensate for a sense of inferiority is not unusual. A guilt complex in proponents of big governments has been recognized for some time."

How Paul explains progressives' destructive attitudes, especially toward the Golden rule?

"It is not unheard of for "intellectuals" to claim that free markets are destructive and the Golden rule mandates an authoritarian state to right the wrongs of uneven distribution of wealth."

It is highly preposterous, but progressives use everything they can to justify their aberrant behavior. Ron Paul stated: "One would not think that a rule asking all to treat others as they would like to be treated could be used to condemn free markets, the only system ever to alleviate famine and subsistence living. Yet this is what has been done."

They've twisted many things, including the Golden Rule, to serve opposite goals and to bring down America. Barak Obama's conversation with Joe The Plumber during the 2008 political campaign had meaning. Obama's aim is to level the United States' productive capacity and attempt to artificially raise the productivity of other nations at the expense of America. One thing he forgets is that our productivity depends a lot on free markets, and the basic freedoms and dignity of American people.

"The Golden Rule is manipulated by progressives to destroy the wealth of the world and thus impoverish the masses." That is their ultimate goal, meaning the masses will have to look on government as their savior. From this impoverished condition, progressives aim to take over the world and humble everyone else.

Paul said it: "It is the moral principle of individual liberty that is vitally needed to achieve the fairest and most prosperous society. "As precious as religious values are when properly applied, a society that agrees on the principle of liberty makes personal religious and social beliefs less threatening."

Paul said it best: "The basic moral principle of individualism emphasizes not only an absolute right to one's own life but the opposite as well: that no one has a right to another person's life or liberty or property. There can be no individual aggression and no national aggression either. This is what the Golden Rule should mean.

"It is outright crucial to grasp that a flawed understanding of what the Golden Rule means can be used to justify violent redistribution of wealth and wars of aggression and must not go unchallenged. It's bad enough that history has been filled with thousands who find themselves in positions of power and don't even pretend to endorse this basic Golden rule principle."

Ron Paul is the first politician to tell the truth about our badly damaged Constitution the failure of men to hold dear the Golden Rule as found in the scriptures or what he calls a moral compass:

Because most men do not understand the Golden Rule, we no longer have this as a moral compass to guide our political system. Thus, we now face the prospect of economic and social upheaval. Without a moral foundation to our political system, it is a free-for-all, and those who understand how to use government power benefit the most. Government is driven by envy and avarice, not the self-interest that drives free markets and is condemned as selfish by the enemies of liberty.

A government without limit, if unchecked, will destroy production and impoverish the nation. The only answer is to better understand economics and monetary systems, as well as social and foreign policies, with the hope that they will change once it becomes clear that government policies are a threat to all of us.

40

Security

Ron Paul believes you should not have to
sacrifice freedoms for security

More than 200 years ago Ben Franklin warned us about it:

"They that can give up essential liberty to obtain a little temporary safety deserve neither liberty or safety."

"The tragedy," says Congressman Paul, "is that the would-be tyrants—with the victims of government fear-mongering who demand ultimate safety—destroy the liberties of those who are convinced that there is no need ever to sacrifice any liberty in the belief that the government will protect us from all harm."

President George W. Bush, like Barak Obama today, was not living up to his sworn oath given by the Supreme Court Justice with hand on Bible—as if that meant anything to Bush—because he put the "safety" of people ahead of living up to his duties spelled out in the Constitution to protect individual liberty.

Caveat: In Bush's case he might have been too ignorant and unaware of reality to know what he was doing. That is a most depricating thing to have to say about one of your former presidents, but in Bush's case it is true. His duty was to 1) uphold the Constitution and 2) preserve our liberty. They are really one and the same duties if you understand the Constitution.

No one, including the U.S. president, can provide complete protection for citizens. "George W. Bush was totally confused on this issue," said Paul. "He claimed his prime responsibility was keeping all Americans safe, not obeying the Constitution. His legal adviser John Yoo said Bush could ignore the law and the Constitution when they interfered with his goal of striving for safety."

I wonder if Barbara Bush taught him that, too? I have met and talked with Barbara Bush and a more outwardly staunch person you will never find. But later I discovered how progressive the Bushes are and lost much of the respect I once had for her for failing to teach Constitutional principles in her own home. Consequently, George got his priorities wrong and the president didn't know how he should behave in preserving, protecting, and defending the most sacred legal document America has. Shame on you, Barbara!

At a recent Tea Party meeting I told a lady I was a staunch Ron Paul supporter. She replied that she couldn't vote for Dr. Paul because she didn't think he could adequately protect her. I was too polite. I should have told her that was not the attitude of true Tea Party members, many of whom had served in the armed forces. "Toughen up, lady. No amount of guns, tanks and planes can protect you from the enemy within—those who destroy the Constitution. If you ask to be protected above all else, you are a lily-livered progressive not fit for freedom. Do you think those original Tea Party participants were worried about their own skins when they defied King George and dumped the tea rather than obey the Stamp Act? You're not fit to call yourself one of them. Had your kind been in power there would not have been a revolution. We would not be a free country and England would still be our master."

In a real way, England—at least the Bank of England and the Bilderbergers—are still our masters because, together with the Fed, they control the money supply and our prosperity. We Tea Party people need to have the spleen to stand up to them, at risk of ou r lives if necessary.

It took mighty sacrifices to make this nation free. And it will require even greater sacrifices—even risk of life and limb—to retain our liberty. That's what I should have said.

Fear ignites a demand to be taken care of. "In a free society," says Dr. Paul, "where depending on government is absent or minimal, any real crisis serves to motivate individuals, families, churches, and communities to come together and work to offset the crisis…Once dependency on government for both rich and poor is ingrained in society, any perceived actual or created crisis will prompt a demand for rescue at any cost."

Paul is right when he says, "The assumption the government can rescue us from all problems and it's not the individual's duty to plan for such unforeseen circumstances, causes behavior changes that magnify all crises through a constant erosion of liberty."

Through private means most Americans can have:

Locks on our doors

Guns in our homes

Private insurance to cover loss

Privately provided alarm systems

Sometimes even private security guards

"The vast government apparatus of national security does not keep us safe so much as [it] threatens our liberties by regarding the entire citizenry as a threat. Private security does not threaten our civil liberties, but government-provided security does."

The authoritarians have this motto: "Don't ever let a crisis go to waste." It only took 34 days from the time 9/11 occurred for Congress and President Bush to give us the damnable Patriot Act. It passed easily by both houses of congress. The people went along because of heightened fear and apprehension.

The Patriot Act:

*Undermined the privacy of all Americans protected by our Constitution

*Caused radical departure from the protections of the fourth Amendment

*Allowed government to seize all our records

*Made all Americans potential terrorists, subjecting us to unrestrained searches by our government "protectors."

The Patriot Act allowed access to library and bookstore records. It redefined and broadened the definition of "lone wolf provisions" such as wiretaps of civilian homes and monitoring of cell phones.

The fact that an extremely unpatriotic piece of legislation was called the Patriot Act tells you something about the arrogance and cynicism that exists in Washington D.C. Congress and the people went along because of heightened fear and pressure to do something. This is no small matter. Before 9/11 we were spending about $40 billion annually on intelligence gathering. A strong argument can be made that this was a total waste of money, since that effort did not prevent 9/11 even with evidence that we now know was available.

Now we spend $80 Billion annually and I doubt we are any better off for it in terms of security. But in terms of erosion and diminishing of our freedoms, we are much the worse off. Says Paul: "Who can say that we are any better off because of this secret spending and interference in other countries?"

The added $40 Billion in security makes possible for the NSA to do surveillance on emails, telephones, mail, and all activities of Americans. There is no privacy left. The U.S. military spends far more than any country on earth. In 2009 the world spent $1.53 trillion according to the International Peace Research Institute Yearbook of 2010. Fully, 46.5 percent of that was spent by the U.S. The next highest expense was by China which was only 6.6 percent of the total. Ron Paul asks how much of that is spent by those countries to protect them against the United States as the perceived threat?

America is a threat? Yes, Ours is the only country that will travel thousands of miles to:

Drop bombs on other countries

To overthrow governments

To station troops

To mess in other countries' internal affairs

The United States is the only country to have used nuclear weapons, and we are surprised that other nations regard us as a threat?

As to the threat of terrorism and wartime policies being foisted upon Americans at a time when Congress has not declared war, this is Paul's observation:

"Conditions [in America] are ripe for some form of dictatorship to emerge. Dependency on government to care for us in all ways has caused the majority of the people and their representatives to act in a way that guarantees our problems will get worse. We are witnessing the destruction of the liberties that took centuries to establish in order to reign-in the kings of old."

On December 31, 2011, President Barak Obama, contrary to what he said he would not do, signed the controversial National Defense Authorization Act (NDAA) into law. This is the same bill that Ron Paul recently to the Patriot Act but with more dire implications. "When the bar is low enough to include political enemies, our descent into totalitarianism is virtually assured," Paul said.

"The recently passed National Defense Authorization Act continues that slip into tyranny, and in fact, accelerates it significantly. The Fifth Amendment is about much more than the right to remain silent in the face of government questioning. Paul continued. It contains very basic and very critical stipulations about the due process of law. The government cannot imprison a person for no reason and with no evidence presented and without access to legal council. The danger of the NDAA is its alarmingly vague, undefined criteria for who can be indefinitely detained by the U.S. government without trial.

It is no longer limited to members of Al Qaeda or the Taliban, but anyone accused of substantially supporting such groups or associated forces," Paul continued. "How closely associated, and what constitutes substantial support? What if it was discovered that someone who committed a terrorist act was once involved with a charity? Or suppose a political candidate? Are all donors of that candidate or supporters of that candidate now suspects and subject to indefinite detainment? Is that charity now an associated force?"

The White House initially threatened to veto NDAA because of the detainee language, saying it would tie the hands of law enforcement officials. But the administration dropped the veto threat before the bill passed the House, as the bill's supporters argued that there were sufficient waivers.

"The president's widely expanded view of his own authority to detain Americans indefinitely even on American soil is for the first time in this legislation codified in law," Paul said. "That should chill all of us to our cores."

The Bill of Rights has no exceptions for really bad people or terrorists or even non-citizens. It is a key check on government power against any person. That is not a weakness in our legal system, it is the very strength of our legal system.

The Obama-sponsored National Defense Authorization Act (NDAA) attempts to justify abridging the Bill of Rights on the theory that rights are suspended in a time of war, and the entire United States is a battlefield in the war on terror. This is a very dangerous development, indeed. Beware.

41

Slavery

Paul supports the rights of all people

John Quincy Adams did not believe in slavery, and neither does Ron Paul. He is anything but a racist, a tag neo-cons such as Glenn Beck and liberals like Bill O'reilly would pin on Dr. Paul for no apparent reason because as a libertarian conservative, by definition, he believes in and supports the rights of all people of all races, colors, and origins. You just need to read his writings to absorb that fact.

John Quincy Adams wanted the slavery issue debated. Following his four-year term as president, he was elected to Congress where he presented the slavery issue for debate, but debate on slavery was banned. Finally, after he and his allies abolished that ban, he began a dialogue. But those who wanted to get rid of slavery were frowned upon and suffered for it politically.

Some people resorted to violence to rid the country of slavery. Others helped protect runaway slaves to keep them from having to return to their owners as mandated by federal fugitive slave laws. Still, the problem persisted.

As Ron Paul says: "You can silence debate, but you can't sweep fundamental moral issues such as slavery under the carpet."

Think of it, slavery is evil. It is the presumption that one human being can own and control another human being like a dog or a farm animal. Slaves were worked and bought and sold without "free exercise of volition."

Paul likens actual slavery to what is going on in America today politically. "...Isn't that also the case with a whole society ruled by a vast leviathan state?"

Congressman Paul believes we got rid of one form of slavery and replaced it with a growing problem of another kind of slavery. Yet today, aren't good and moral men and women being confronted with that same kind of social pressure and ostracizing peer pressure concerning other issues?

Laws and mandates against home schooling are:

Laws that force onto us

- The draft

- Confiscatory taxation

- Speech controls & Regulations

- Regulations designed to control our social lives

- Any number of impositions of life. Libtery, pursuit of happiness and and property laws and issues

"The issue of government ownership and control of society is also a moral issue. And no matter how much the elites try to shut down debate, the issue is not going away. Paul mentions two courageous abolitionists, William Lloyd Garrison and Wendell Phillips, champions of the movement to give blacks equal rights like whites. Unfortunately, it took a Civil War to settle the issue, resulting in the death of more than 600,000 Americans.

Paul blames our refusal to settle the matter peacefully as John Quincy Adams wanted to do, by way of Constitutional Amendment. Basically, abolitionists were separatists, believers in secession.

Garrison said:

By the dissolution of the Union we shall give the finishing blow to the slave system; and then God will make it possible for us to form a true, vital, enduring, all-embracing Union, from the Atlantic to the Pacific—one God to be worshipped, one Savior to be revered, one policy to be carried out—freedom everywhere to all the people, without regard to complexion or race—and the blessing of God resting upon us all. I want to see that glorious day!

There was never a discussion that the states didn't have a right to leave the union. But many still believed that this industrial state would work to eliminate slavery. Ron Paul praised Wendell Phillips: "Phillips paid a high price for his long effort to rid the country of the scourge of slavery. Throughout all of early America he was scorned and ridiculed. He never wavered in his convictions and saw himself as an agitator and reformer whose goal was to force the American people to face the issue of slavery as a moral imperative."

This next statement displays the spirit behind Ron Paul: "Wendell Phillips demonstrated how one individual with determination and truth on his side can influence an entire nation."

Paul believes Phillip's "unyielding efforts based on strong beliefs in pursuing justice are an example of character rarely found in today's society.

Phillips inspired the masses as an agitator:

What does an agitator do?

1) He proselytizes

2) He does not write the laws

He changes people's opinion so that great and significant social change can be achieved. Congressman Paul also points up the importance of the strategic planner for social change: he is not a politician subject to the chicanery of the politician forced to accommodate both sides.

He does not speak in double talk

He does not move slowly in one direction or another

He deals with precise ideas, not fuzzy compromise

He appeals to common sense, personal conscience and fairness

Ron Paul compares the role of the strategic planner with the politician who is just the opposite, who is one to "tinker around the edges, while the revolutionaries—either for good or for evil—work to change the fundamentals of the political structure once the agitators have prepared the way."

The role of the strategic planner for social change is ignored when conditions seem to be stable, but when a crisis hits, the views of those who argued for change are suddenly listened to. Quiescent years can go by, requiring great patience and determination and education. Ludwig von Mises is an example of the above determination:

He never yielded to the establishment that scorned and punished him for his views. "Today, he is a hero to millions for his willingness to stand firm on his principled defense of the free market and explain how it benefits the masses."

Paul said we live in an age where the current system is being challenged for philosophical and practical reasons. I'm not referring to the Constitution, but of America's retreat from the Constitution and Bill of Rights pushed by progressives and the current system of special interests, lobbying, big money in politics, political skulldrudgery, power plays, and contempt for fair play and operating by moral rules and those given us by our Founders.

"Its [big government control of a nation's economics] failure is becoming more evident every day," says the Congressman. There have been plenty of agitators and reformers for decades expecting and warning of lowering living standards brought on by regimentation of the social and economic order.

"They have offered freedom as the practical alternative. Fortunately, their voices are growing louder and it is reasonable to be hopeful that our times will prompt a sea change in America's understanding of what the role of government ought to be."

Tyrannical government must be turned on its ear in 2012:

Ron Paul believes the climate looks quite hopeful for social and political changes to come out of hibernation.

He urges all of us to become agitators for liberty. Otherwise, we end up in a permanent state of slavery to party bosses and the "swampy", creepy, secret way of doing things in Washington including midnight closed one-party sessions and the ramming down our throats of bad laws like Obamacare which was passed in a very clandestine fashion.

42

States Rights

When did we get it wrong? States were supposed to be more powerful than the federal government.

Under the Tenth Amendment States have rights to retain all powers not explicitly delegated to the federal government. Under the Constitution, it is Washington whose powers are limited, not the states and the individual. As Ron Paul puts it, states act as a kind of bulwark over the overweening federal government.

The Constitution protects the independence of each state by setting up a limited relationship with those people in Washington. But over the years progressives have stripped states of a lot of power.

Paul notes the relentless history of progressives in Washington passing more and more legislation that aggrandizes D.C. at the expense of the states, such as in education, welfare and especially Obamacare.

"An attack on the very notion of states rights," said Paul, "is an attack on the form of government that the Founders established.

The Ninth and Tenth Amendments have failed, but no words on paper can adequately protect the freedoms of the states or of the people from despots. How can states reject the tyranny coming out of Washington today?

1) Interposition

2) Nullification

3) A new Constitution

4) Secession

Interposition is the doctrine that a state, in the exercise of its sovereignty, may reject a mandate of the federal government deemed to be unconstitutional or to exceed the powers delegated to the federal government. The doctrine denies the responsibility of states to respect Supreme Court judgments with which they do not agree. See Bush v. Orleans School Board. However, the Supreme Court rejected this doctrine of interposition in Cooper v. Aaron.

Nullification is the state or condition of being void; without legal effect or status. Dr. Paul stated that as the economy continues to deteriorate and our freedoms are further undermined, there will be a lot more talk about getting out from under the heavy hand of central government and its failures.

"Those who charge that defenders of state sovereignty are un-American and unpatriotic reflect an ignorance of history and the Constitution."

Those same people do not criticize the breakup of the Soviet Union or the principle of self-determination.

The doctrines of interposition and nullification been used throughout history to some degree. For example, many runaway slaves were not pursued by the law in some non-slave states, and rightly so. Those charged with protecting slaves were frequently not found guilty by juries, despite overwhelming evidence to the contrary.

Ron Paul is adamant in his abhorrence to bad law. Refusal to enforce bad law against American citizens by oath keepers would have been helpful and moral during the civil rights struggle during the nineteen-fifties and sixties. The beatings and arrests would not have occurred if law enforcement officials refused to comply. If the military personnel involved in the Kent State killings on

May 4, 1970, had refused to participate in the shooting, a much better outcome might have been reached."

Nullification was used by the South Carolina legislature in 1832, It was in ordinance opposing the viciously unfair Tariff Act of 1828. Congressman Paul believes that if that ordinance had been entirely successful in nullifying the act that became known as the of Abominations, the odds of avoiding the bloody Civil War would have been enhanced. The tariff caused prices of manufactured goods to soar and imports from Britain to disappear. Paul said that this made it more difficult for the British and others to buy southern cotton. These were good reasons for the south to be furious, and thus the conflict between North and South escalated.

Jury Nullification: This is a Constitutional term meaning juries have the right and the duty to judge both the facts and the law, according to Paul. In today's courts. juries try the facts only, and the judge is arbiter, or final decider, of the. Law. Today, if a judge learns that a particular juror believes in jury nullification, that juror can be removed.

Throughout the land people are questioning the progressive desire for the governed to feel dependent on government. With the amount of debt Washington has amassed, who would feel safe in the arms of that kind of master? It is common knowledge that a significant segment of society cannot make it with the current tax system. Many have joined what used to be called the Black Market or underground economy. That is where people disguise their earnings and purchases by a system of barter or operating off the books.

The more authoritarian a society gets, the more desire for people to do business in the Black Market. At the height of the Soviet Union's power, the underground economy thrived. I was visiting the Soviet Union 1961 and saw foreigners selling hard-to-get American clothing such as Levis on the sidewalks to Soviet citizens for cash. They, in turn, would mark them up and sell them to local people on the Black Market without taxes or records.

Paul believes that as things get really bad in America, it will drive them to adhering to federal mandates—especially, once it's clear that the feds no longer have the ability to bribe and coerce the states into submission. "The federal government will become less significant and maybe inconsequential when the empire collapses and the welfare state becomes irrelevant."

Paul is right. America is a welfare state in the midst of a currency crisis. "Just printing more dollars and running up more debt can no longer provide the pretense of a cure. It only makes matters worse."

Under these conditions, if interposition and nullification do not work, the relationship between the states and the federal government could start to look more and more like secession.

Do not be overly encouraged. The government will use brute force against the people in an effort to hold the state together.

Lincoln did. He had what he termed his Happy Farms. They were nothing less than concentration camps for Lincoln political enemies. This is why there are Americans today who do not share the love of this man many of us call the greatest president America has ever had.

However, Lincoln is remembered for finding a way to pay his army and navy to fight in the Civil War and hold the nation together, despite terrific odds. How did he find the money to pay the troops when banks wanted as high as 36 percent interest? He printed Green Backs. These are government issued money not backed by Gold. I advocate that we should do that again. If we did, we could save the country, turn around our monetary system and defeat the Fed. If Ron Paul is elected, this is precisely what he will do, along with permanently expelling the Fed and bankers like it by legislation.

That last statement about Lincoln's concentration camps may dismay you, but it's true. Look it up in history books. Lincoln and FDR's concentration camps could be used as precedents for a dictator today to detain—and, thus, kill—millions of American citizens, particularly, those conservatives who do not support such an evil man.

By signing the National Defense Authorization Act (NDAA) on December 31, 2011, President Barak Obama made himself America's first dictator.

You say you don't believe that statement? Do your reading. Obama would invoke his power to jail anyone he wanted under the new NDAA. How a Republican Congress could pass such a wretched bill is totally beyond me. We must thoroughly clean house this fall, throwing out every Congressman and the president who voted for that bill—a law so damaging to the Constitution and to our lives and safety that one must cringe with horror just to think about it.

In my 2011 political thriller *The Exterminator*, (soon to come out under another title, *Murder By Executive Order*) I write about another president, Conroy Drake, who set up a string of concentration camps in every state for that very purpose. You can find this exciting novel at Barnes and Noble and Amazon.com. Visit Don White's landing page at **http://bit.ly/tjGsUc** or **http://whitewriters.blogspot.com**

"Welfare programs will disappear long before the domestic military presenceto 'keep the people safe' from the dangers of anarchy is humbled," said Ron Paul. "It is a shame that it could come to this, but power is indeed corrupting and intoxicating to those who want to rule others for their own good."

We hope it doesn't come to this. All we are demanding is that the feds adhere to the Constitution and the Tenth Amendment. But many Americans have become docile, accepting anything their caretaker government gives them. Like sheep, they have been too long complacent and tolerant of government abuse because, as the smartest GOP candidate for president, Ron Paul, puts it, "Our wealth seemed to be guaranteed and government benefits became more desired than independence and liberty."

The Congressman, whose words ring true today just as Patriot John Locke's words resonated three centuries ago, said that now with the enlightenment gained from the financial crisis, "people are making up for their complacency. The anger expressed by the Tea Party is a sign of how serious the conditions have gotten. And we're still in the early stages of the crisis."

Socializing an economy on the brink of total collapse can hardly be the answer. Ron Paul and his many followers believe the stakes are extremely high, but the real answers are obvious. But still we ask, what is stopping most progressives from seeing the danger in which America finds itself? John Locke had the answer:

"It is one thing to show a man that he is in an error, and another to put him in possession of the truth." John Locke

43

Statistics

Don't Rely Too Heavily On Statistics

Statistics are seriously limited in at least three respects, said Ron Paul:

The validity of statistics depends entirely on the way they are collected, what's collected, and how they are presented.Statistic do not interpret themselves, and so their meaning is easily manipulated by politicians.

Statistics tell us nothing about cause and effect. Thus, they really do not address the crucial public policy issues about which we should be asking.

Governments of all political persuasions resort to statistics to find evidence that supports their cause. Paul said that sometimes statistics are used for political spin, but often their use results in gross distortion of economic reality. "Statistical distortion used in combination with political spin doctors can temporarily deceive the market, but only for a limited time."

The Fed stopped reporting M3, the money supply statistic, when it revealed too much evidence of the flawed Federal Reserve policy. "For a long time M3 was revealing the Fed's policy of excessive monetary inflation during a period when most economists of all persuasions now agree that interest rates were held too low for too long."

Ron Paul said government unemployment statistics are virtually worthless in describing the seriousness of the economic downturn. If a discouraged person quits looking for work, he or she is not listed as unemployed. This is wrong. It distorts the numbers; and it's always distorted to favor an incumbent president or congress. As is the case today, when a significant number of unemployed persons say they have quit looking it distorts the unemployment figures, as it did in late November and early December, 2011 when the unemployment statistic dropped like a dead weight from 9.3 percent to 8.5 percent unemployment. That was very misleading. It came two or three weeks before Christmas and we know that after Christmas retail buying will lag and temporary workers will become unemployed again.

When Ron Paul wrote his book Defined in 2010, he says unemployment was actually 20 percent when it was reported at ten percent. How is this possible? It all depends on the way you collect and report. The Gross Domestic Product figures are always favorite numbers of financial markets. They are used by political pundits and politicians to brag on an improving economy.

"The politicians want credit and also help for the next election." But GDP, even without fudging, is a flawed statistic," he says. "In a recession the government increases spending by borrowing, by printing money, or by raising taxes. Regardless of what the money is spent on, this will raise GDP."

What people don't readily realize is that borrowing, printing money, and taxing are negatives for the economy, something not revealed.

In reality, higher government spending lowers economic growth. That's why the statement is true that you can't spend yourself out of a depression or a recession. It's a negative factor. But tell that to the progressives. They believe you can spend you way out of anything, just like some drunkards believe you can drink yourself sober.

Paul observes that blowing up bridges overseas and rebuilding them increases our GDP by counting bombs and planes produced, but none of it increases our national wealth. "It would be more accurate to subtract government spending from GDP than adding it to that total," he said. "I tend to be suspicious of all government statistics because the really harmful ones are never mentioned."

The Congressman said he uses statistics to see what damage government is doing. "Statistics are used to provide bogus 'scientific evidence' that government is doing great good for the country. It is no better than a fortuneteller who pretends to know all truth by looking into a crystal ball. The more you swim in an ocean of governmental data, the more confused and disoriented you can become."

44

Surveillance

Big Brother Has Reams Of

Data On Each American

If you've seen the television suspense show called *Persons of Interest,* you will find that some genius has invented a machine to photograph everyone everywhere 24 hours a day and to record trauma or situations where someone is going to die or come into harms way, usually due to no fault of his own..

It's the stuff of which science fiction is made. But you probably don't realize that even without all that sci-fi stuff, each of us is photographed several times a day. We are caught on film or our data is collected.

- Getting money from a cash machine

- Buying things at the convenience store

- Shopping at the grocery store

- Merely by driving around in a parking lot

- When we browse on line

When surveillance is done by the private sector, it raises few problems. It is known to serve a social purpose and perhaps leads to more security and better service. Private security cameras on private property can be quite useful. Many homeowners have installed inexpensive cameras on their homes so that they can check on uninvited people coming to their door or to the rear of the house. Government should not play a role in this. We are all happy to see private citizens filming police brutality, or other out-of-line behavior. Today's video cameras have caught more police misbehavior than at any other time.

Government cameras are another story. Challenging these cameras in court is usually out of the question. They are out of control at:

Traffic lights

Roads and streets

Buildings

Paul says the government excuse is always the same: they are providing safety for the people, but unlike the private sector this is not really believable. Government is fanatical in protecting its own secrecy.

Under the Patriot Act, private cameras are fair game for government inspectors, alphabet agency operatives and intruders. Our own cell phones, cameras, and the Internet, including the computers where we keep sensitive data, can be subpoenaed and taken by government ops without as little as a receipt.

Potentially, everyone can be a perceived threat to America. Money managers, hedge fund gurus, and even stock market traders can be, and are, under the all-seeing eye of the government. Since the Patriot Act, any bank deposit of $10,000 or more is under government agency scrutiny. Moving large amounts of money around from account to account, or merely to earn the most from an investment, is closely watched by big brother.

In reality, America is under siege. But it is not by the Taliban or al Qaeda, it is by our own government. Privacy laws have been dumped in favor of a promise from the government that we are, somehow, now more secure and safer because of all of this.

45

Taxes

Oliver Wendell Holmes Had It Wrong

Like it or not, Oliver Wendell Holmes, a well known progressive, had this to say about taxes: "Taxes are the price we pay for the cost of civilization."

Frankly, neither Ron Paul nor Author Don White appreciate that statement at all. Mr. Paul believes that policy has cost America dearly. Paul proclaims that civilization comes about through economic, moral, and social development. A precondition for civilization to exist is freedom.

Civilizations have thrived without taxes for periods of time throughout history; but liberty is the most important ingredient for civilization to thrive.

"The whole notion of running the economy and the world and paying for it by forcibly extracting taxes from productive individuals violates the principle of natural rights," said Congressman Paul. When carried on to an extreme, this destroys the means of production and the wealth of a country.

America didn't get an income tax until 1913, and it was because of President Woodrow Wilson, a very progressive politician. He had war in mind and the only thing he could come up with to pay for it was a system of income taxes. Before that, federal revenue came largely from tariffs, a form of taxation that didn't directly attack citizens' property rights. Income taxes were embedded in the Sixteenth Amendment.

Ron Paul laments that after property could be taxed, "the whole structure of the relationship between the citizens and the government changed. Now we had a different philosophy at work, one that presumed that government had a claim on the productive efforts of every worker."

Taxes started at low levels, but as government gradually expanded in the twentieth and twenty-first centuries, spending began to exceed taxes taken in, so something had to give. Either we had to cut some of the government programs that taxes were paying for, or we had to raise the level of taxation. Guess which of the two changed? Increased spending necessitated more taxes until when you look at America today, spending on government projects has never been higher and, for demographic and other reasons, grinding taxation is projected to continue to rise because demands on welfare and other benefits continues to climb.

The following is not from Ron Paul's chapter on taxes, but Don White's. It is highly germane, representing thinking and ideas of many Americans. They are suggested by Dr. Paul's writings, but do not come directly out of this Ron Paul tax chapter.

How did America do so well for the first one hundred forty years of its existence without the progressive income tax law provided for in the Sixteenth Amendment by President Wilson and other progressives? The answer is that before Wilson and Teddy Roosevelt, father of the Progressive Movement in America, we listened to George Washington and other Founding Fathers regarding "no entangling treaties" and other obligations. We had no appetite for foreign wars and intrigues or for welfare spending. If it wasn't in the Constitution, it wasn't in the independent makeup of people living two hundred years ago. Have today's people today gone soft?

Welfare and wars are the two great drivers of higher taxes. It took America one hundred fifty years to realize it wanted more from government, that America suffered because it didn't look at all like European nations, an utter falsehood. To the elites, war became a convenient way of spreading their One-World progressive ideas across the globe by policing the world in the name of national security at a huge cost of lives broken by loss of limb and psychological injury and loss of national treasure.

To satiate the aggressive demands of progressives, America became the biggest producer of war materiel in the history of the world. Hitler and World War II were stimulants toward the current hawkish American attitude. In concert with the Rothchilds of the world, banks funded and America built the largest military machine on the planet.

Since banks don't fund anything without interest, I should say we built this vast military complex with American debt, on the backs of our grandchildren yet to be born. Who could be so immoral? It was the largest banks on the globe that want a one-world empire and domination over all peoples of the earth as their goal. They are aided and abetted by a bellicose, power-hungry Pentagon, and self-avowed corrupt progressive politicians.

There has never been a military force in the history of the world that even remotely rivals America's military power. Yet, today we have politicians like Obama, Romney, Gingrich, Perry, and Santorum who in 2011-2012 stood out as war hawks, praising the principle of America's overwhelming power at any cost. It encompasses perceived geographic, economic, and political needs of America with the emphasize on the word "perceived." During the last hundred years politics grew to encompass geography, demography, and economics, especially with respect to the foreign policy of this great nation.

One cannot be U.S. president or secretary of state without a clear understanding of these things. Military and foreign policy are interrelated and dependent on each other. There never has been a stronger nation than America. Even ancient Rome would look with envy. The new geopolitical responsibility of the United States encompasses outer space, the oceans and the sky, an empire boasting some 900 foreign military bases manned with missile-delivery-capable drones and other armaments, necessary ingredients to prevail at modern warfare. But this huge geopolitical industrial-military complex doesn't come cheap.

The United States still has a lower overall personal tax burden than the typical advanced economy in

Europe. But the gap isn't as big as you might think, and it may be poised to shrink as the pace of federal spending ticks upward. Here's a look at how Americans' tax burden ranks against that of citizens of other countries, and why it matters.

In 2006 U.S. personal taxes were relatively low, fifth lowest in the world after Mexico, Turkey, Korea, and Japan. How do US tax rates compare with those in other nations?

The average American pays wage-based taxes that are similar to what Britons pay—and not much lower than France. Japanese citizens enjoy the lowest rates among the Group of Seven large industrial economies, or G-7. This includes national and local income taxes, plus payroll levies such as the employee share of Social Security. The president and Congress have robbed Social Security of some $112 billion in payroll contributions because politicians find it popular with voters to give wage earners what amounts to an average of $1,000 a year tax break by waiving those taxes, thus depriving Social Security of any funding.

Over the past fifty years, politicians have been so greedy and vote hungry that they have completely depleted the Social Security fund. President Lyndon Johnson was able to claim he balanced a budget in 1969 because his administration robbed the Social Security coffers. But that wasn't the first time SS had been off budget. Currently it is off budget and there is no money in the trust fund.

Social Security trust fund assets consist of Treasury securities. This means that the taxes collected under the Social Security payroll tax—beginning in 1935— are in effect being lent to the federal government to be expended for whatever present purposes the government requires. In this indirect sense, one could say that the Social Security trust funds are being spent for non-Social Security purposes. However, all this really means is that the trust funds hold their assets in the form of Treasury securities.

In the Social Security Act of 1935 the income from the payroll tax was to be credited to a Social Security "account." Benefits were to be paid against this account, but originally there was no formal trust fund as such. Taxes began to be collected in January 1937 and monthly benefits were to be paid starting in January 1942 (later pushed forward to January 1940). So the payroll taxes were just credits in the Social Security account on the Treasury's ledger under the initial law.

Wage and payroll taxes are just part of the overall U.S. tax picture. Add in sales taxes, capital gains taxes, property taxes, and corporate taxes, and the US sends 28 cents of every dollar of output to the government. As of 2010, that still matched Japan for the lowest ratio of tax revenue to gross domestic product (GDP). Among G-7 nations,. France and Italy were the highest taxed nations.

2009 OCED

Personal Taxes as GDP percentage

Why is tax policy important?

Why view it globally?

The US is headed toward what finance experts call a "fiscal train wreck." If left uncorrected, current trends would force the government to spend a growing amount to service the national debt. That debt burden, or the tax hikes that might occur because of it, could substantially slow economic growth.

Or, the alternative to heavier taxes could be—as Ron Paul suggested—drastically cutting spending. His plan saves a trillion dollars the first year, primarily from overseas. That means the savings by bringing our troops home and closing down foreign bases—especially in places like Germany and

Korea where they have thriving economies and are capable of defending themselves.

Paul would also cut five departments of government and abolish Obamacare altogether, along with hundreds of silly rules shackling American businesses and tending to curtail domestic investment in plants, equipment, and especially in new businesses which normally create jobs. In four years Paul projects he could cut the IRS completely, leaving corporate taxes, tariffs, excise taxes and other taxes to shoulder the load of a much smaller government as America did in the Nineteenth and early Twentieth Centuries. No longer would the U.S. be the policeman of the world. Foreign aide would be cut and the country would be placed on a normalization process.

One giant step toward healing America would be close reigns or a complete takeover or abolishment of the Federal Reserve System. America would again print it's own "greenbacks" without interest and for the benefit of every American citizen.

Bilderbergers and banks of the world would be literally "kicked" out of America and would become persona non grata. Many of their officials should be tried for treason, but probably won't, for fraud, and extortion and sent to prison for the most massive Ponzi Scheme we have ever seen. The fraud associated with the Fed makes the Bernie Maddof ponzi scheme look like kids' play in comparison.

What categories of taxes do Americans pay?

Income

Property

School

County

State

City

ExciseI

nheritance

Sales

"The greater the government taxes, the greater the need, since government management is inferior to individual management, and the money is always misallocated," said Dr. Paul.

"As long as people believe the nonsense that taxation is a blessing and any objection to it means opposition to civilized society and is morally wrong and unpatriotic, we will see a continued decline of civilization. The early American patriots understood the destructive nature of taxation."

Examine the above country-by-country chart of taxation. A study would reveal that the higher taxing countries are usually the most inefficient nations. That would mean that Scandinavian countries plus France, Belgium, and Finland—all of which find themselves on the top of the tax chart for most heavily taxing their people—are also some of the most unproductive and inefficient. Mexico, Turkey, South Korea, and the United States are the most productive and efficient.

The rationale is this: "People tolerate high taxes for a while, when they have wealth, but as the tax burden increases productivity falls and the only answer for it seems to be higher taxes. According to Congressman Paul, if the people can no longer tolerate higher taxes, government merely borrows and creates new money. But the inflation tax is paid with higher prices. "The whole process destabilizes the political system and eventually becomes a threat to civilized progress."

Paul believes it does irreparable harm when citizens get into the mind set that their taxes are fairly paid for government services and are, therefore, necessary and a fair exchange because government is compassionate.

"Depending on government to take care of us sharply diminishes any desire for assuming responsibility for ourselves."

Government spending is unwise. It interferes with the market on how capital should be allocated. The only people who benefit are the politicians, bureaucrats, and the special interest recipients of government spending programs. The country becomes poorer, generating anger.

That anger boiled over in November, 2011 when Hudson Institute writer Peter Schweizer's new book *Throw Them All Out* was aired on November 13, 2011 on the CBS TV program "60 Minutes," alleging that members of Congress were guilty of insider trading. Congressional hearings were held and those involved, of course, denied they were enriched by insider trading.

One Congressman got early news due to his congressional position that a road would be built in the middle of Illinois. He went out and purchased some 324 acres of land near where the proposed road would go, six months later selling it and pocketing a $2 million profit. If you want the Congressman's name, read Schweizer's book.

Members featured in the report, including Speaker John Boehner and House Minority Leader Nancy Pelosi, have denied any wrongdoing and their staffs have given analyses of their investments to ethics watchdogs to back up their rebuttals.

The issue, however, has gained political momentum and legislation seeking to clamp down on any possibility of insider trading by members of Congress was introduced in November, 2011.

The bill is called the Stop Trading on Congressional Knowledge (STOCK) Act of 2011.

Supporters of the bill argued that there is little legal restraint on what they deem congressional insider trading.

The bill would prevent members of Congress, their staffs or anyone who works in the executive branch from making investment decisions based on nonpublic information they gather on the job. But like any other bill, this one will cost Americans more than not having the bill. Someone must be hired and assigned to the task of regularly researching wrongdoing and bringing it to the attention of the Department of Justice. And then, as is frequently the case with Attorney General Eric Holder, you have to get him to prosecute the wrongdoing. If he won't, to get action you will have to expose Holder and the wrongdoer in a congressional hearing and start impeachment proceedings.

House Financial Services Chairman Spencer Bachus was also featured in the "60 Minutes" report and in the book. They alleged that he made investments during the 2007-2009 financial crisis while he had access to briefings and information that was not public.

Bachus strongly denied the charge, including one that he made investments betting General Electric Co's stock would go down. "The book [*Throw them All Out*] is absolutely false and factually incorrect," Bachus claimed in a letter to the book's publisher. Is it? The author Peter Schweizer of the Hudson Institute is standing by his words and is not uncomfortable at all because, apparently, this book is well researched and accurate.

America political leadership is finally waking up to the fact that the corporate tax rates businesses face in the U.S. are way out of step with our major economic competitors. In 2008, for example, Ways and Means Chairman Charles Rangel proposed cutting the federal corporate tax rate from 35 percent to 30.5 percent. While a 4.5 percentage point cut in the federal corporate tax rate may sound significant, it may not be sufficient to meaningfully improve the competitiveness of the United States.

In 2011, the average combined federal and state corporate tax rate in the U.S. was 39.3 percent, second highest among OECD countries to Japan's combined rate of 39.5 percent. Lowering the federal rate to 30.5 percent would only lower the U.S.'s ranking to fifth highest among industrialized countries.

Corporate taxes in America have gotten intractably high—now overall the highest in the world because Japan in 2010 lowered their rate to about five percent. Unless there is a revolution of some sort, or a drastic change via the ballot box, America's economy will continue in a pattern of decline, with jobs shipped overseas and a prosperous China or, possibly, Russia to compete militarily with America and its western allies once again.

When banks control the U.S. president, they also control this vast military-industrial complex and dictate that this powerful nation continue to be the policeman of the world, protecting military and banking assets and interests working in concert with the Federal Reserve System and its banks in not only building most of the world's armaments, but lending the money to do so from the world's most powerful organizationcomprised of politicians and bankers. It is known as the Bilderberg Group. This group largely controls America's foreign and domestic policy, not the people or the politicians, which is a common misconception.

It was discovered that if big banks and industry could control who ran for president through liberal lobby money, it could control who was elected president and largely direct economic, monetary, and foreign policy of the most powerful nations on earth.

Let's get back to Ron Paul's views:

1) Funding of Schools By Imposing TaxesIsn't Working

More and more parents are moving their children into private schools because the quality of educations available in public schools has greatly dropped. "Our public schools today are grossly inefficient and very costly. Paul says the costs are spread around in ways that do terrible economic damage and waste resources."

2) Government Health Care Is Wrong

"Government control of health care paid for by the government has not been successful, and yet the American people are demanding more of the same. Increased taxation hardly provides a more modern and civilized system of medicine." What would happen to health care if government would step aside? Paul responds that health care dollars would just be spent elsewhere and more efficiently without corporate and government bureaucrats placed between the doctor and the patients.

Once we rid ourselves of unnecessary rules and red tape, the entire system doesn't fall apart. Ron Paul reminds us that "a system that is absent a huge bureaucracy and high taxation is not anarchy. Rules of contract, property rights, honest money, and voluntary exchanges with the necessary bankruptcy laws provide order and efficiency."

Financing wars

The greatest uncivilized consequence of giving government blanket authority to tax is to finance senseless war and to provide largesse to the military-industrial complex. "Using funds from a system of taxation and inflation, and wars being fought without declaration have created a dangerous situation for all of us. Our presence around the world in more than 130 countries could not be sustained without the power to tax."

Paul is very critical of our policy of preventive war around the world. It makes the world a perilous place—a threat to civilization.

The following statement by this great conservative, Ron Paul, tells the entire story: "Taxation is realized only by force and threat of force. This always means a threat to civil liberties and the Constitution. Freedom suffers from it. Yet, the freer a country is, the more productive and civilized it becomes. Taxes are a hindrance to both.

"We've seen government grow during the Obama administration. The bigger the government, the more tax revenues required, which threatens economic and political stability."

If I were to describe Ron Paul best I would call him a minimalist. He said it: A minimalist approach to government and taxation places an obstacle to wars abroad and waste at home. The big spenders in government are the same people who throw off Constitutional restraint. "They cannot be champions of personal liberty and at the same time promote government interference in our economic and personal lives."

I'm sure he is talking about all six of the other candidates for the GOP presidential nomination when he says: "Those who champion military interventionism overseas cannot maintain credibility when they talk about personal liberty and balanced budgets. There is a limit on the amount of taxation that the people will tolerate, but the appetite for government spending is never diminished.

That is why borrowing and debt [spending] continue and grow exponentially, ultimately leading to the inflationary tax to be paid at a later date. Paul contends that we are doomed if we continue to believe that paying for civilization through taxation is a wise purchase and the only way to achieve civilization. It's a bad deal for the cause of liberty.

46

Terrorism

Terrorism is non-state violence

committed for political reasons

Terrorism is not new, as Ron Paul points out. It's been going on in the United States from day one of the founding. Paul traces the word "terrorism" back to the French Revolution.

"The United States has bombed dozens of countries in the name of retaliation, but innocent people in those countries are more likely to think of U.S. actions as a form of terrorism."

Isn't it odd? When the U.S. occupies a country, we might call resisters to occupation "terrorists," while they call it patriotism. America most strongly opposes terrorism against innocent persons. Ron Paul observes, "If Americans do not feel safe abroad, or are willing to subject themselves to humiliating searches at airports just to avoid it, our very liberty is at risk from the terrorist threat."

How do we analyze the problem?

We discover the roots of terrorism to understand the actions. If we want to end terrorism, first take a good look at what causes it, especially that which is of a political nature.

Irrational reasons for terrorism:

Religion

Desire to slaughter innocents

U.S. foreign policy

Congressman Paul discounts item one and two. He claims it is all about

Our foreign policy

Our involvement abroad

Our troops in Saudi Arabia

Our subsidization of the border

Expansion of Israel

Our sanctions

Our war belligerence in other countries

"This is not to say that changing these policies would engender a universal brotherhood of peace and love, but it is to draw attention to the undeniable reality, the plain fact, that most terrorism is not irrational, but rather driven by specific grievances."

Before "plunging" into more wars, Paul concludes that we would do well to examine each of those policies and consider their costs "that make bad situations worse."

Ron Paul suggests that groups like al Qaeda wouldn't exist if countries like America didn't occupy their nations. What is America's foreign policy?

We send more troops, sending a signal that there will be no tolerance for dissent.

We fight terrorism by exacerbating the very reason for that terrorism. Thus, we increase the violence against us. In Dr. Paul's view, whenever the government wages war on anything—poverty, drugs, illiteracy, etc.--it is likely to make the problem worse.

Since wars enhance the power of the government, it has no incentive for discovering the problems created by its wars. Candidate Mitt Romney said he would listen to the generals in the field before taking action. But isn't that one of the problems—we listen too much to the Pentagon rather than listening to our heart and intellect?

If the answer were always more war, yes, by all means listen to the generals. But it isn't, so throw out that "solution." More wars merely mean more spending and more wars to follow. It's a never-ending cycle—unless you elect a president who goes to war only when another nation attacks America. Wars, themselves, enhance the power of government. For many Americans that idea is too simplistic and counter intuitive, but that doesn't make it wrong.

Why make war, in the eyes of bureaucrats?

They enhance electability of war hawks

An excuse for bureaucratic expansion

They bring in more revenue

Wars are excuses to violate civil liberties

Threat of war is an excuse to whip up the people into a state of fear, thus being easier to control. That is precisely what happened following 9/11 when George W. Bush introduced us to the Patriot Act which Congress, also in a state of haste and fear, readily signed on to.

"I have doubts that just as with the war on poverty and communism, the government desires to win," said Ron Paul. "The incentives are exactly the reverse: the worse the problem becomes, the more excuse there is for government power."

The above would be an astounding statement if it were not true.

Paul quotes from a study by Robert Page. He is a researcher at the University of Chicago who did a study of six years and 2,200 terrorist attacks. The study was based on ten thousand records from publicly available databases. His conclusion:

"We have lots of evidence now that when you put the foreign military presence in, it triggers suicide terrorism campaigns...and when the foreign forces leave, it takes away almost 100 percent of the terrorist campaign." This statement and study validates Paul's quarter-century-old statements. "Invading other countries is a bad idea, especially if the goal is to stop terrorism; quite the opposite will be the result."

Governments are incapable of even providing good internal security: Airlines are a good example. Their security is best left to private security firms. They should be required to deal with their own security needs. Armored car companies protect money and no one worries about it.

In conclusion: the way you decrease terrorism is to bring all the troops home. That is Ron Paul's intention if elected president. The GOP war hawks like Gingrich, Romney, Bachman, Perry, and Santorum laughed when Ron Paul mentioned bringing home the troops. Laugh on fuzballs:

"Fools laugh at others. Wisdom laughs at himself." -Osho

If we are really serious about destroying terrorism we would:

- Withdraw troops from foreign countries

- Not go to war if it's an aggressive war

Look at how our policy incites desperate people to take extreme measures of retaliation against U.S.-sponsored political violence.

Neoconservative Republicans and most Democrats don't know how to reduce terrorism or to save a trillion dollars a year by bringing our boys home and closing expensive bases abroad. They work on the fallacy that America's strength comes from its military power, rather than from the liberty and freedom of intelligent minds.

What a waste it would be to elect any but Ron Paul.

47

Torture

Information extracted from alleged

terrorists by torture is rarely of value

There is no difference between Obama and Bush in saying torture is okay and of "great value" in keeping America safe. When Americans endorse torture, they think they are endorsing rough treatment of militant terrorists guilty of committing violence against us.

The Constitution forbids torture. Laws of other countries and international law forbids torture. America tortures innocent people not charged with crimes or convicted of a crime, including American citizens.

Bush started calling it enhanced interrogation techniques. America has been brainwashed into believing that our national security depends on torture and that it has worked

People die during torture. Some commit suicide. Now we read that some who our government said committed suicide were killed by the CIA. President Obama refuses to prosecute agents who tortured innocent people and committed suicide. The CIA has destroyed all records regarding the heinous crimes they committed with complete impunity.

In a "free" country, knowledge of these crimes would be reason for the media to come forth with information, charging malfeasance and demanding a Congressional investigation. But America is no longer that kind of "free" country.

According to Dr. Paul, many terrorists captured during the last ten years was due to paid informants. "Accusing your enemies of terrorism gains you a bonus check from the U.S. taxpayers and lets the agents of torture have a field day." The feds quickly claim that those captured were taken outside our country and are, thus, enemy combatants not deserving habeas corpus or other Constitutional rights.

While only a couple of the people captured were American citizens, the precedent was set for a time when anarchy reigns and the government wants to arrest you and me and treat us like enemy combatants too. The Congressman believes that the day may come when Americans may become vulnerable to the charge of supporting a so-called enemy terrorist "for merely challenging our foreign policy and claiming to understand why thousands, if not millions, of Muslims around the world like to do us harm."

"It looks like secret prisons, clandestine rendition, unlimited detention, and torture are all still part of our policies. No effort has been made by the new administration [led by Barak Obama] to investigate charges of misconduct in the previous administration. Protecting state secrets is just as strong a policy today as it was in the last administration."

Paul believes that the record is clear that getting any valuable evidence from so-called "enemy combatants" is very rare. Those being beaten will say anything their tormentors want them to say to avoid further bodily harm. A more humane method of persuasion yields far more positive results than torture.

"The image of Americans torturing prisoners at Abu Ghraib and Guantanamo circulated around the Muslim world has done unbelievable harm by the hatred it generated against all Americans. It's going to take a lot of time to alter that sentiment, and it won't happen without a change in our foreign policy and our assumption that we can arrest anybody anywhere in the world at will."

At least one prominent general is against America torturing people. He is General Barry McCaffrey: "We tortured people unmercifully," he reports. "We probably murdered dozens of them during the course of our Middle East wars, both the armed forces and the CIA."

Paul says the ACLU and many news services estimate that at least 100 detainees died as a result of torture while in American custody. Our government has tried to downplay those deaths as suicide. So far those responsible for this travesty have not been held accountable.

Due to this, it is not a stretch of the imagination to accept torture of gang members in America. Will this attitude spread? Paul believes the door has been opened for it to spread to all Americans if things get tough enough.

"The clandestine activities of the CIA, FBI and all sixteen intelligence gathering agencies is something that is so massive and secret that even presidents have a hard time understanding to what extent they operate. To oppose their authority is considered by many in D.C. as unpatriotic and un-American.

This is not a good sign for America. We lack an understanding of civil liberties at all government levels. Remember, you will be on the right side of the truth if you oppose torture. Don't be afraid to voice your opinion verbally or in writing about this heinous misuse of government power.

48

Trade Policies

Ron Paul makes a great case

against protectionism and tariffs:

Protectionism is related to military Keynesianism in that many supporters of militarism are also champions of sanctions and blockades. True, a lot of protectionists thoughtlessly push protective tariffs purely as a job program meant to protect noncompetitive domestic industries and do not support them for military reasons. But what they don't accept is that trade and friendship diminish chances of war with other nations, and protective tariffs are actually harmful to the American consumer.

"The moral hazard to protectionism is that the less efficient will not be motivated to become more efficient in order to survive. Complacency and inefficiency set in."

Do you consider sanctions and blockades acts of war? Congressman Paul does. He believes they are very dangerous. Some people today [December 2011] want the United States to oppose Iran's suggested blockade of the Strait of Hormuz, to stop Iran's Navy from restricting traffic in these strategic waters.

Radio Free Europe on December 22, 2011 wrote the following:

"A hard-line Iranian newspaper considered to speak for Iran's supreme leader has come out in support of closing the Strait of Hormuz in the Persian Gulf, the world's most important oil-shipping lane, as punishment against countries that have sanctioned Tehran over its suspect nuclear program. A December 13 editorial in "Kayhan" asks, "Why has the Islamic Republic of Iran not used its unchallengeable right 'till now, when there is a conspiracy of imposing sanctions against our country's oil?"

The piece comes a day after an Iranian lawmaker reportedly said the country's military was planning to hold drills to practice closing the vital shipping passage. The news agency ISNA quoted deputy Parviz Sorouri as saying, "If the world wants to make the region insecure, we will make the world insecure."

Paul is against these sanctions, in fact sanctions of any kind. He says sanctions were a prelude to our unwarranted and illegal invasion and occupation of Iraq. "There's reason to believe that the same will happen from our trade barriers against Iran."

He states that the worldwide condemnation against Israel came from blockading the Palestinians in Gaza, an inhumane and dangerous policy. The result has been to make the region much more dangerous. It has undermined the Israeli-Turkish friendship that has served both east and west for decades. Paul is convinced that our interventionist policy in the Middle East is neither good for America or for Israel.

Unfortunately, many members of Congress believe that strong sanctions are an alternative to war, rather than a precursor. Blockades can only be enforced by physical force, moving the two opposing parties closer to war. "What they fail to see is that blockades can only be enforced by violence and killing," said Paul. "Iraq is a good example. Sanctions were imposed through the 1990s and then the real war followed." Trade and friendship move opposing parties in the opposite direction.

"I consider myself the most radical free trader in Congress," said Paul. But I do not vote for international trade organization [WTO, NAFTA, CAFTA, and others], the Congressman said.

"The process by which these agreements are passed is flawed." Usually, Congress takes a fast-track attitude and congressional authority over this is transferred to the executive branch. "The office of the president negotiates with other groups of other countries the details of how to lower tariffs or gives permission to retaliate against another member for unfair trade practices."

He says the only way the executive branch should be involved is to draft a treaty to be ratified by the Senate. If the president is required to get two-thirds of the senate to agree, this is a problem, but it's easy to get a majority to agree to fast track legislation.

"Since the Constitution is clear that Congress has the responsibility for foreign commerce, I don't believe the President should even attempt to regulate foreign trade by treaty." Do you now see how these trade agreements become instruments for international government entities—like NAFTA and the CTO— to regulate trade without explicit consent of Congress? Paul believes with rules they literally "undermine our national sovereignty and that of our states as well."

He says too often these rules can be beneficial to large international corporations while at the same time harming, ignoring, or being detrimental to small companies unable to defend themselves against the giant bureaucracy serving the special interests.

Countries that won't lower tariffs hurt their own people more than anyone else, since tariffs are a tax. "If a foreign country subsidizes a product and goods become cheaper than our own, it's an economic boon for the domestic country. Our country then has more money left over to increase our standard of living by purchasing other products."

The consumer is the "special interest" in a free market—not the protected corporation or union. Many of the strongest supporters for sanctions against such countries as Cuba, Iran, North Korea, and Iraq are many of the professed free traders in Congress "who get their credentials by supporting all free trade agreements." He states that this mocks the position that nations that trade with each other are less likely to go to war. "The truth is," states Paul, "that some may well understand this and believe in this principle, but it's war they seek. Too often that is what they get."

Both Paul and this author believe that America's stopping all flow of oil in early 1941 was a significant factor in the attack on Pearl Harbor later that year.

Dr. Paul defends free trade. Whether it be tennis shoes from China that cost $20 if manufactured there and $100 if made in America, why punish the poor for the sake of protecting domestic industries?

Some people complain that China uses "slave labor." The answer to that is that those are jobs that the poor chose to take. Yes, China uses low-cost labor, but all you need to do is compare the current standard of living using these low-cost jobs against the standard of living under communism that they had a few years earlier.

What we here in America must understand is that much of our labor is priced higher because of minimum wage laws, unemployment benefits, and compulsory unions, "while prices are pushed higher as a consequence of excessive regulation, taxation, and government caused inflation."

Paul is sure that protectionist measures don't solve the problems. All they do is maintain the status quo that keeps America from being competitive in many industries.

49

Unions

Unions gained a foothold in America

during the Great Depression of the "Thirties

The National Labor Relations Act of 1935 was at that time the most important piece of labor law ever. But it did something stupid. It passed minimum wages, a law responsible today for much unemployment. A lot of workers today would rather just have a job than see companies living on the margin during the terrible recession of 2008 through 2012 (and continuing) than have to lay people off because they can't afford to pay a minimum wage.

That bill also formed the nucleus of all labor regulations that would follow, and all would form an impediment for small business owners, taking many of them out of business during tough times—again adding to unemployment that was staggeringly high in 2011 at just under nine percent today, not counting another ten percent from those who have simply given up looking for a job.

One of those bills was called the Wagner Act. It deepened the depression rather than help Americans get back to work.

Arguments Against Unions:

They increase the cost of goods and services

Unions make the company less competitive

Unions dictate who can work for the employer, an unfair intrusion into ownership and management of a private enterprise. Unions sponsor violence against nonunion firms.

During strikes of union shops, nonunion shops are in jeopardy. By striking, sometimes the laborer gains legal force over the employer, forcing the firm to go out of business. Economically, in the long term, union strikes hurt union members.

Union strikes are bad for everyone. They have resulted in legalizing "featherbedding" which means a union worker who does nothing must be paid by the company. This was common in railroading, driving costs up, making shipping and transportation more expensive.

Unions have indirectly been responsible for a loss of standard of living for millions of people by virtue of higher prices people must pay for union-shop goods and services.

Labor laws intended to protect workers have caused services to end, such as home delivery by milk companies.

Labor laws helped to prolong an economic mess in the 1930s.

Some states have passed "right-to-work" laws, meaning a worker is not required to join a union if he doesn't want to. But many more states have passed liberal laws requiring that everyone in a particular labor segment must join a union. This is unfortunate because it eliminates freedom of choice from the labor market place.

I side with Ron Paul: "What good is it to mandate a $75 per hour wage (I was making a buck eighty per hour at the Associated Press) if there are no jobs available at that price. What good is a minimum wage of $7.50 if it significantly contributes to unemployment?"

Here's the other side of the coin

It's heartless and unfair not to force "fairness" on the ruthless capitalists.

Dr. Paul's answer to that is that "true compassion should be directed toward the defense of a free market that has provided the greatest abundance and the best distribution of wealth of any economic system known throughout history.

"Once power is given to government to set wages higher than the market rate, it also has the power to fix wages at lower rates as President Nixon did in 1971 with wage and price controls."

Who has used wage and price controls?

Truman

Roosevelt

Nixon

Compulsory unionism, protected by government by a majority vote, distorts the true cost of labor and violates the Constitutional principle of minority rights.

Two more things wrong with compulsory unionism:

Making workers pay dues to be represented by any organization they disagree with is hardly fair or just.

Coercing businesses to accept contracts with unions at the risk of being closed down is not a voluntary agreement. Workers who are willing to work at a lower than union wage are subject to violence by militant union workers. It is best to have a government that caters neither to unions or business

Ron Paul believes "that in a free society unions would not be banned, but the employer would only deal with unions voluntarily." In a free market economy, labor becomes scarce and the businessman must seek the best workers by offering the highest wages.

According to Paul, the best way for unions to gain clout is for the free market to thrive and the good workers to become scarce, creating higher demand and higher wages.

Sometimes unions and big business cooperate, as they did when the Defense Department under Donald Rumsfeld took the M1 Tank building contract away from GM in 1977 and awarded it to Chrysler to help them stay in business. Congressman Paul said we didn't need the M1 Tank. It has never been used in combat. "It was merely a military industrial complex boondoggle to serve the interests of big industry and big labor and to save Chrysler. This type of spending contributes significantly to our bankruptcy and the drain of capital resources away from productive enterprises."

Pros and Cons of the Chrysler Deal:

Pro: It kept Chrysler in business

Con: It set up the unimaginable bailouts of today

Con: Worst of all, it set a bad precedent that government's role is to bail out companies. It misdirected resources. It also conditioned Americans to accept that in tough economic times the role of the U.S. Congress is to bail out corporations by protecting unearned profits and high union wages.

Now, sadly, many Americans believe that spending on military weapons—even on ones we don't need—"can help a company or even an entire economy recover from government-caused downturn."

Unbelievably, Paul says he is hearing in Washington that the only way to get out of recessions or depressions is to go to war—as FDR did.

Who supported the Chrysler bailout?Big labor

Big banks

Big business

Big Government

Laws/ actions designed to help a small segment of workersMinimum wage laws

Mandating union contracts (closed shop contracts)

Davis Bacon rules

The above hurt unprotected workers. But long term, excessive wage demands actually hurt labor by creating unemployment. "It is no coincidence that Detroit workers suffer more severely than those who are employed in the states where arbitrary union power is held in check by right-to-work laws. High wages are great, but if there are no jobs they become meaningless."

In the real world, it is workers versus companies. Workers strive for highest wages while companies strive for maximum profits. If left to the market, consumers decide:

Consumers vote constantly on:

    a. Which products to buy

    b. Quality

    c. Service

    d. Price

Efficiency and productivity determine Success, or Failure. Things that grossly distort the market process and contribute to the mal-investment initiated by Federal Reserve policy guarantee that in the correction, wages must come down.

What are the factors in play?

Prevailing wage laws like Davis Bacon

Coerced union wages

Dictated minimum wages

In a free market, all contracts between workers and companies must be without government interference. No one is forced to work, and no one is prevented from quitting. Government has no power to force obscene wages on the taxpayer and no one has a contractual right to strike and hold the taxpayer hostage.

"It seems strange that the idea of voluntary associations and personal choices are so readily accepted by both progressives and conservative persuasions, yet when it comes to setting wages it's assumed that only an all-knowing, all coercive government has the wisdom to know what the proper wage should be," observes Ron Paul.

Artificially high wages significantly contribute to unsustainable debt in government and business, making the Federal Reserve generated business cycle that much worse. Paul believes that ignorance in economic affairs, blind acceptance of government regulations over the free market, reflects an unwillingness to recognize and defend the principle of individual liberty.

When the goal is liberty, prosperity flourishes and is well distributed, Ron Paul said. When economic equality is the goal, poverty results.

49

Zionism

The Jews Were There First

Ron Paul writes a beautiful, hopeful beginning to this chapter that I will leave by merely saying that the Israelis have an historic claim to their Palestinian land, despite the fact that Israel was under Jewish rule only about 170 years.

According to Historian Juan Cole, the Jews were there all the time. That includes the 1,191 years they were ruled over by the Muslims. It doesn't seem fair that merely because a nation occupies another nation that when things are divided up later that the length of time of tyrannical control of their land should be counted toward ownership.

But then, you and I are citizens of a nation that has conquered and held territory, later completely releasing it to the captive citizens. For example South Korea, Germany and other European nations that we liberated, Japan, the Phillipeans, and other island nations. This lack of dominion doctrine was almost unheard of in the annuals of ancient warfare.

The Israelis were there before the group that now likes to call itself Palestinians, before the Samarians who were transplanted by the Assyrian king from Babylon from five regions during one of his conquests. They lived in what became Samaria, former ten-tribe territory which included Jacob's well.

Wikipedia reports that Jerusalem had been fought over sixteen times in its history. During its long history, Jerusalem has been destroyed twice, besieged 21 times, attacked 52 times, and captured and recaptured 44 times.

Another time when the conquered Israelis were carried off to Babylon in one of many waves of Babylonian sieges the Samaritans merely moved across town to more choice real estate without legal title into vacant Israeli houses, and certainly far before the more recent warring Arab tribes and Muslims came to Jerusalem in the sixth century. It wasn until 610 that the Temple Mount in Jerusalem became the focal point for Muslim Salah (prayers), known as the First Qibla, following Muhammad's initial revelations. That wasl ong before the

Christian Crusaders laid siege during the height of anti-Semitism in Europe.

History leaves few witnesses to testify of the force rendered when the Greeks, Romans, Muslims, Christian and the Babylonians looted, killed, and kidnapped. Reportedly, Christians killed and displaced all but a thousand Jewish families of a 300,000 population.

But it was the Babylonian Empire that disrupted the land of Israel most, marching them off to a land we now know was at the center of present-day Iraq. Then, it was a beautiful land known for its powerful leaders and its hanging gardens; but today only dead space exists where once this mighty people's industry and energy prevailed over the world.

This land is now devoid of signs of the history that the Prophet Daniel wrote about. If he could only view it today, he would find no evidence of this historical place's once glorious history, just miles and miles of sand, covering scant evidence of anyone having lived there. Babylon is but a dot on a map today, a thousand-mile trip from Jerusalem, walking the meandering dirt highway the Jews were forced to take, a poignant reminder to the world that in the end, despite what might appear to proud mortals as staggering odds, God prevails over all, despising evil and honoring his prophets. This proves once again that man is little more than dust of the earth. The partitioning off of Israel came because of some strong pressure in the US to get the matter approved by the UN's Security Council. Ron Paul is not a believer in the United Nations.

He knows that had the UN not acted and reacted to activists who wanted some "legal" confirmation of Israel's existence, the entire area around Israel might be a friendlier place for several reasons.

Until the UN got involved:

Immigration to Israel was mostly voluntary, and gradual. It was accomplished with due respect for existing land titles. Zionism, during the first forty years of this movement, was not about taking land by force or militarism.

"A continual peaceful transformation would probably have occurred except for the political actions after World War II in which the United Nations turned a local and demographic issue into an international and highly politicized one," said Dr. Paul.

Zionist Movement Positives:

1) It enabled Jews to recapture their language in record time

2) Heightened consciousness of Jewish identity and purpose

3) Helped restore the Jewish faith as a living presence

Zionist Movement Negatives:

The political agenda has been divisive for the Middle East and the world. The entire mission of creating a homeland might have been accomplished without the use of force

One of the first decisions made by the UN was accepting the Security Council's recommendation in 1947 to partition Palestine. That same year the UN partitioned Korea. By June, 1950, "blessed" by UN resolution, America was back at war, siding with South Korea against the Soviet Union and China which supported North Korea.

"Considering the number of lives lost and the money spent, it doesn't say much for the UN's peacekeeping efforts or our own foreign policy of the past sixty years," opined Paul. Congressman Paul has studied the problems that this small piece of land called Israel has caused." Paul said, "There should be a statute of limitations on ancient claims of ownership. [But] Those still in possession of titles to land and homes should not be cavalierly dismissed out of a sense of justice." I am one who doesn't agree with Paul regarding Israel's claim for this territory.

He notes that, despite the fact the fighting has gone on for thousands of years, "there have been examples when people were left alone for relatively long periods of time," living side-by-side with their adversaries without incident because there was less government involvement. But for a surety, when Muslims ruled over Jews they were particularly harsh and charged them heavy taxes and barely let them live and exist as a separate people.

"Different religious groups were quite capable of getting along together peacefully," Paul argues. "Intermarriage, regardless of religious beliefs, was not unusual. My advice: Leave the young people alone and they'll find out that they prefer lovemaking to war making. And are more anxious to get along with one another than the older generations who stir the pots of war.

"Give government any kind of foothold and it will figure out a way to force or incite young people into war making. The old saying is true: 'Old people and governments start the wars and young people must fight and die in them for all kinds of cockamamie reasons.' "

Congressman Paul is very unhappy with what he sees as uneven treatment we give Israel

compared to Iran over nuclear weapons. Israel has 300 nukes, Iran none. "The fact that Muslim nations become annoyed with this policy is written off by most in the West by charging anti-Semitism.

Within Israel politics there is a great deal of debate and diversity of opinion about this issue. Paul says the Liberal party in Israel often raises questions about the apartheid conditions that Palestinians are subjected to and that even Israel newspapers are willing to discuss this issue openly. But it is essentially not permitted in the United States.

The good doctor who has brought more than 4800 babies into this world said that former U.S. President Jimmy Carter is now persona non grata in some US government and accademic circles for raising the question in his most recent book, : Peace Not Apartheid.

Regardless of the above, Ron Paul's position is the same as it is with any other country:

Dr. Paul favors a non-interventionist position. His position is consistent with that of the American Founders. Paul would like a policy of peace, friendship, and trade without intervention in any country's internal affairs. Unlike the views of all other presidential candidates, his coincide with the Constitution.

America has been known to hinder friendly outreaches by Israel to its neighbors in the Middle East and her use of nuclear weapons. Here in the West we believe Israel listens to us not because they agree with America's stated objectives, but because we generously subsidize Israel. "Israel is not a truly sovereign nation as long as it depends on getting U.S. permission to do what it sees is in her best interest."

Paul says that "if Israel were to be so bold as to attack Iran without explicit approval of the United States, we will be blamed anyway. If war spreads to include Iran, we will be in the middle of it as long as today's conditions persist." He believes the net effect would be a plus for Israel if we stopped all aid to foreign countries. Paul doesn't feel that will ever happen because we must protect our "oil" and to do that we must remain in the territory for an indefinite time period. We also support Arab nations with money, and many of them are not going to become democratic. Our strong aid to Israel eliminates any desire they may have had to work out their own differences with foreign nations.

The author of this book believes, like most Americans, that during this time of terrible recession, America does not have money to be aiding anyone. Most Americans today feel that all foreign aid, including to Israel, should be stopped. And even when we're back on our feet again, we should not resume these "bribe" payments.

But Ron Paul is further to the center than that viewpoint. In addition to lack of money, for other cogent reasons America should discontinue policing the world and doling out large sums of money? When we do achieve a peace agreement, no matter which countries are involved, it usually costs America plenty.

Example: The Camp David Accords between Israel and Egypt cost the American taxpayers billions of dollars "in perpetuity." Our presence at peace tables discourages Israel to work out its own problems. This bought peace has cost Americans more than $150 billion since 1979, yet friction still remains.

Artificial peace treaties hinder the need for all involved to rely on commerce and trade to improve the standard of living for both sides and to work out their differences locally. An alliance between Israel and moderate Arab nations may well have been developed to deal with Saddam Hussein. That type of solution would have been a blessing to all Americans.

Instances and reasons how right wings in America and in Israel have failed:

The threats toward Iran and the sanctions come at the constant urging of the Israeli rightwing government and their supporters here in the United States. But Israeli dissidents who speak out against Israel's foreign policy are rarely quoted in America.

Any opposition to Israel in the United States is rarely reported in our liberal media. For these and other reasons, Paul opines that despite how emotionally charged and historically controversial the Middle East is, logic is not likely to prevail and allow a peaceful, bipartisan solution anytime soon.

Misplaced religious passion of the three great religions which are theoretically supposed to worship the same God prohibits the universal sharing of the Golden Rule, love for our fellow man, and the desire for peace.

Congressman Paul is convinced that if the U.S. were to stay out of the Middle East, both economically and militarily, it would be most helpful because a neighborhood solution would more likely occur "without us stirring the pot and jeopardizing more Americans being killed in wars yet to come.

The author adds his name to those who believe that this policy would be in the interest of Israel, the United States, and world peace.

End Notes

My goal is twofold: to do all I can to aid Ron Paul in his bid for the presidency and to publish and broadcast his constitutional views because they are true and right.

If Paul wins it will be a miracle, noting how fraudulent Republican state politicians do all they can to elect their choice, probably Romney, even to the extent of failing to count votes coming in from all district of some states. This leads to but one conclusion: voting in the GOB primaries is rigged and fraudulent.

Some of the emerging countries used to call for US help in monitoring their first elections. We obliged, but now it's our turn for some help. Voting in the primaries is rigged. It's just, plain and simple, not fair, especially to Ron Paul. It all started with the debates where Paul was asked maybe two questions while all of the other nine candidates were asked (and able to answer) seven or eight questions. Then it moved on from there where today such national media as CNN isn't even interviewing Ron Paul along with Romney, Santorum, and Gingrich. The media no longer has an embedded reporter on the campaign trail with Ron Paul as they do with the other three.

Who is driving this total lack of fairness? Well, this is just an opinion but I would say it comes down from those who pick our candidates in the first place, The powerful inter-nation Rothschild bankers who stand to lose if Congressman Paul becomes president because he would bring our troops home and commit this country to reducing it's policeman of the world involvement.

We all know that the country that assumes that responsibility also must pay huge sums of money to engage in unnecessary wars across the globe. That militarized country must protect and defend the isles of the sea and every continent on earth with the strongest and largest navy and air force it can buy. It must supply and man our "empire." This consists of more than 900 bases across the globe. All of that costs money, big money.

When America invests in the military, it borrows the money to pay for it by asking the Fed to print more money and, in turn, the Fed gets our US Treasury Department to print up IOUs or Treasury bonds that we sell on the open market adding to our already more than $16 trillion in debt including the onerous interest burden, that will be borne on the shoulders of our grandchildren because, quite frankly, America is broke.

If Ron Paul doesn't win the nomination—and frankly, it looks unlikely as of April, 2012—all is not lost.. He has helped educate the American people about some very important principles. Dr. Paul is the most intelligent and patriotic candidate of all. We would sorely miss his reasoned mind and efforts at helping America understand the importance of Constitutional law if he completely left the political scene as he has promised to do if he loses his bid for the presidency..

For many, this would not be a particular tragedy. But if you're a libertarian you are likely saying "What a shame." If you are a Tea Party conservative you should be sorry, except the more I look into the Tea Party the more I see that they have been hijacked by the neo-cons and that isn't good because they believe sanctions and war are the answer to every problem. Initially, Ron Paul provided most of the insight for that movement, whether many of these impassioned Americans realize it or not.

Dr. Ron Paul's intention was to follow Washington and Jefferson's suggestion: go to Washington for a short time and return home and assume his original obstetrics profession. Dr. Paul didn't want to stay.

In fact, he was the first Congressman in America to write a bill proposing term limits and that was in the 1970s. He proposed congressional term limits multiple times during his twenty-four-year service to this country.

His term limit bill was always defeated, so when he saw that people in Washington wouldn't budge on their moderate and liberal ideas he decided to stay and fight. Freedom-loving people across the nation are glad he did. Congressman Paul knew he could make a difference and he has. What would this country be like without conservatives like Ron Paul in the House of Representatives?

When democrats heard that Congressman Paul was retiring some were ecstatic. Their minds sent up victory balloons and rockets. They were glad this feisty medical doctor-lawmaker would no longer be on the scene writing books and pestering the liberals with sound thinking on a variety of issues, all opposing progressive demagogy and big government.

This is the same Ron Paul who ran for president as a libertarian in 2008 and lost, a man who is again running for president in 2012—this time under the GOP banner.

Luke warm critics might say that if the past is any indication of the future, he can't win in 2012.

Nonsense! He wasn't supposed to win in his first bid for the House of Representatives, either, when he ousted a democrat incumbent.

Something told me to offer Ron Paul my help, but how? By reducing his latest book down to the nuts and bolts of what he believes and entice those "kids" who didn't know any better last time to read and understand Ron Paul's glorious ideas. Then I hope they will believe and take action at the polls. Now I just need a long list of emails for these people.

America's youth and old alike need to hear Congressman Paul's message—that what America needs most right now is fewer, not more, rules, which make it almost impossible to run a small business. Seventy percent of new job growth in America today is by small businesses, but we have chained them with rules and regulations that make it almost impossible for them to compete with foreign countries. Reduce the size of government. Ron Paul can fix all of that. he would spend less and balance our budgets. He would cut the fraud and waste out of government and stop those senseless wars. The others say they can do some of these things too, but we know they are not true conservatives and don't have the staying power.

This is part of Ron Paul's program. He can fix America, fortifying us economically, socially, and militarily with real clear conservative values that will liberate the nation from the heavy yoke of big government and years and years of wars of aggression that God warns will lead to our downfall.

Ron Paul is a moral man. Those government officials and candidates for president who want more wars of aggression and more and more military spending have lost their compass, lost their inspiration. We can no longer afford to be the world's policeman. Morally and physically bankrupt, America can no longer be expected to throw money at this problem and that.

Fortunately, Americans of all persuasions are awakening to that fact. They know that failure to correct our course, to fix the monetary system, and to downsize government in a meaningful way will result in more of the same. But it's time the rank and file American woke up and learned this lesson as well and became an agitator for good. Speak up, America!

As a weak nation, inflation will soar, jobs will continue to be lost to foreign nations, and we will become vulnerable to alien powers as we currently have fallen prey to countries like China from whom we had borrowed trillions of dollars each year, money that we currently have no way of paying back.

If we fail to change directions in the 2012 elections, which must include ridding ourselves of the socialist-Marxist presence in the White House that has openly vowed to level America economically and militarily to that of a third world nation, freedom will never return to American soil and the spirit of America will be lost.

It's unfortunate but true that many Americans don't realize how bad the situation already is. This once independent group of colonies that were brazen and bold enough to cry for liberty and throw off the awful yoke of King George became the darling of the world. It won liberty on the battlefields of Lexington and Concord and throughout this land. Because of the U.S. Constitution and a liberty-loving people, America became the mightiest, bravest, most productive nation on earth.

But there is a worm eating away at its insides today. That worm is called socialism, Marxism, big government, entitlements, and overarching illegal president-inspired executive orders on every conceivable facet of our lives. The worm will continue to tear us apart unless we vow to stop this insidious ninnyhammer that has entangled, slowed, crippled, and strangled every facet of government and social life.

The nation is already badly weakened, and things will continue to get worse under the yoke of big bank gangsters and Wall Street imperialists who have helped create big government to further their international interests at the peril of American liberty.

Congressman Paul has decided to retire from the U.S. House of Representatives after 12 terms so that he can concentrate all of his efforts on winning the Republican nomination for president. That's the good news.

Ron Paul is a rare gem, a highly educated and intelligent common-sense man whom I, a former Democrat (almost 50 years ago) and past supporter of moderates like Mitt Romney, now vow to support. What was I thinking? I should have gone full tilt in support of Ron Paul much earlier. And so should all Americans.

If it took me a while to see the light, there must be plenty more out there that need re-educating on Ron Paul. I am convinced that my short version of his book, Liberty Defined, is just one of those things that could help do that.

Like conservative Senator Barry Goldwater (R-AZ) before him, Congressman Paul is a devout patriot who believes in conservative concepts. .

Barak Obama's plaintiff cry must go for naught: **"If you love me pass my bill?"** Obama was talking about the continuation of an unnecessary thousand-dollar Social Security tax break that he saw helping him get re-elected. It was a bill that Republicans in Congress opposed, then, ineptly, passed. Then does anyone wonder why I am calling for a wholesale House cleaning, of even many of the weak-kneed Tea Party congressmen who voted with Obama.

Obama said the above stupid lines? But what has he done to warrant our love? Just the opposite—he hates America so he deserves our scorn. He has done everything he could to bring America down. He shames America in front of foreign governments. He is not a cheerleader for America's Yankeeism or exceptionalism. Quite the opposite, and he has become a public embarrassment like the other day on an open mike in South Korea when he promised Russia's former president Dmitry Medvedev he would need some "space" until he got re-elected and then he indicated he would give away hundreds of our nukes, and for what?

In a negotiation, you seek something in return. But this weak president, Barak Obama, forgets how Russia supports Iran and opposes our sanctions and our desire to stop this terrorist-loving regime from getting and distributing nukes to all their terror-loving pals.

Iran is not a responsible nation, and yet our "old friend" Russia turns a deaf ear on our plea for help. All the while Obama is bowing and sucking up to Medvedev wasting what could be a strong bargaining chip. Who's to say that like his parents, Obama isn't just an old communist, himself, after all? Otherwise, why all the "love" for this former communist regime which, itself, is quite repressive even yet to its people.

Vladimir Putin got back into office by fraudulent means and you can bet Obama has been watching him and will pull every dirty string and use every crooked device to defeat a squeaky-clean Mitt Romney.

Obama's message is flawed and no amount of jokes, lies, and big-tooth smiles can make honest Americans believe we are better off today than we were at the end of 2008.

And what about those other two orators, FDR and Woodrow Wilson? FDR gave us bigger government and the welfare state and Wilson gave us the progressive income tax and the Federal Reserve System in 1913, and he broke a campaign promise to keep us out of the war by doing just the opposite. Within days of his second inauguration, like the progressive near-dictator he was, he took us into World War I.

The Fed and Obama's profligate spending has just about wiped out the country's prosperity and any chance we have of escaping the economic chaos it created. Fed Chairman Ben Bernanke is like Wilson. Now he wants to spend billions more in another of what he calls "Quantitative Easing" or QE3. His unstated goal is to wipe out the value of the dollar.

His latest fiasco was to lend Europe $600 billion of our grandchildren's money. Money that will be lost down the deep dark hole of Keynesian deception and will do absolutely no good because it won't get to the people but will be devoured by those wicked banks that already hold everyone living in a central bank nation hostage with compound debt-filled, interest money—capital designed to collapse countries and economies at will. There you are, George Soros, the Fed is doing it for you.

Our primary political goal is to defeat Obama with Ron Paul who is the only candidate out there who understands the Fed's evil power over us, and how to remove the shackles of debt and despair with which Obama and Ben Bernanke have shrouded America—the only candidate who promises to remove the chains of the bondsmen and liberate us, our children, and our grandchildren from the awful Federal Reserve and its global power malaise.

Congressman Paul's mantra also includes bringing home our troops—not all but 3,000 of them, but all of them—cutting the outrageous spending, balancing the budget, abolishing communist-inspired rules and regulations that stymie new business and job creation, and winning back our place as the most free country in the world. Today, due to Obama and his progressive friends in Washington, America ranks ninth behind socialist Canada on the Heritage Foundation's list of free nations.

That's atrocious! What happened to "The Land of the Free?"

No one can tell me that having a bunch of communists and socialists in the White House writing onerous rules is good for the economic and spiritual health of our nation.

On the political trail, at times Ron Paul may struggle with liberal press appeal. That's because he tells it as it is and the media is owned by the big banks, remember?. That's why those very same liberals and their moneyed friends hate him. But Americans liked three other men who spoke their minds, Democrat Harry Truman and Republicans Barry Goldwater and Ronald Reagan; and they are learning to like Ron Paul, too. You see, America's love affair with Ron Paul is just beginning.

Could Democrats and Independents become passionate about Dr. Paul? Of course, many already are. Not that Congressman Paul isn't getting even hard core Democrats to vote for him, because of his sound approach to economics, broad foreign policy appeal, distaste for expensive wars of aggression and the grief and misery it brings our troops, many of whom come home hobbled and wounded mentally and physically, and his stand on many issues that Democrats share. But he has enemies, too. He doesn't expect to be all things to all people—leave that to Santorum, Romney, Gingrich, and Obama—and he's just too honest to be all over the map with his convictions.

One liberal moaned about Paul's delivery, "You think you're listening to Gomer Pyle." He was referring to Dr. Paul's bubbly, gentle, rural auto mechanic panache. Home folks love that style, but he gains less affection from non-libertarian elites. That TV persona was portrayed by popular American singer/ television actor Jim Nabors whom we all loved in the fifties and sixties.

Today's voters are attracted to glitz and pseudo intellectualism with some lies and jokes to cover the untruths thrown in here and there.

The ready quip was one of Ronald Reagan's secrets of success. But unlike Obama today, Reagan was an honest man and people could count on him. People can also count on Ron Paul.

Some elites prefer young, tall and handsome presidential timber with a clearly resonating voice, despite the fact those candidates have a nasty habit of over-promising and rarely delivering.

It happens all the time. When we elect a dishonest person we wake up one fine morning to find that he or she has ghosts in their closets that can't be fixed with timely smiles and jokes—things that almost got Bill Clinton thrown out of office.

Inevitably, we deserve what we get. Dishonesty seems today to be one of the chief shortcomings of winning White House candidates, but that's not a Ron Paul trait.

Paul may seem somewhat verbose; at times his lines may even lack punch, quips and wit, at least from a Madison Avenue point of view. It is because he is not Ronald Reagan at the podium, nor would he like to be. He's Ron Paul, plain and simple—but with a far superior intellect than any of the others including Reagan—a tell-it-as-it-is man who writes his own speeches and doesn't use a prompter that I can tell. I thought he really "brought it" in front of his large Iowa straw poll crowd and in earlier appearances and in later speeches.

In the Arizona debate, moderator John King of CNN asked Ron Paul why one of his political ads depicted Rick Santorum as "a fake." Calmly and with his eyes firmly fixed on Santorum, who was standing right next to him, Dr. Paul said he called Rick Santorum a fake "because he is a fake." There wasn't any hesitation or disembling on thepart of Dr. Paul.

The audience ate it up, but Paul wasn't pandering to the audience or to anyone because he meant it. The audience couldn miss the genuine honesty of this great man. No, unlike all the rest, Ron Paul wasn't pandering.

Ron Paul doesn say something like that unless deep down in his gut he means it. Rick Santorum is a fake because he masquerades as a conservative, yet it is well known that he was one of the biggest spenders in the US Senate, certainly not an economic conservative, and neither are Romney and Gingrich.

Paul is the only true conservative running. Will America wake up to that fact?

The others can praise themselves three ways until Sunday over their love for America and their social conservatism, but the closest they come to being conservatives is the word Neo-conservative. Merriman-Webster defines neo-conservative as a former liberal espousing political conservatism.

That word, neo-con, works well with Romney, Santorum and Gingrich. In order to meet the stiff criteria of a true conservative like Ron Paul, you must be militarily, socially, and economically conservative.

I would add a fourth criteria, willingness to live and govern strictly by the US Constitution as a strict constitutional constructionist and to follow the Founders advice concerning warfare, taxes, freedom, liberty, and the economy; and emphasize by actions one's love of God and country.

Obama immediately flunks the course. Except for Ron Paul, none of the GOP contenders served in the military. In summary, they do not qualify in the "love of country" criteria unless they donated a couple years or more to non-church or community service as Romney did when he went on a 30-month church mission to France when he was a young man. No Doubt, All GOP Candidates Love God

Ron Paul and Mitt Romney exhibit their love of God and staying power, persistency and greater faith in religious principles, perhaps too, by the higher amounts and regularity of donations freely given to their churches or to to their communities and the length of time donating and attending. For a long time, Dr. Paul has only taken half of his congressional salary.

Rick Santorum and Newt Gingrich, while professed church men, were "money-grubbing" lobbyists. When they weren't representing constituents as Senators or representatives, they were drawing large salaries from mega firms that crave the mind-bending, deceitful feats accomplished by lobbyists in D.C.

Let me be clear, not all lobbyists are evil or even come close to it. They have a job that they see as important, one of being an historian or educating lawmakers to their products or their way of political thinking. You be the judge as to whether the above two lobbyists were misusing their former positions for personal gain, and whether that's the kind of person you want residing in the White House. But me? I vote against them.

Draw your own conclusion. I'm sorry about those 34,000 lobbyists now working in D.C. or in that vicinity that may become annoyed at my "money grubbers" statement. Not all of them fit that description, of course. But their unusually high salaries are indicative of something. Each would attest that their abilities gained while representing the people can and are now used to influence votes on bills in Congress. This kind of influence is worth a lot of money and in my mind that is a despicable form of labor because it hurts or mitigates against American voters influence, or at least cheapens it. Pitted against what special interest money can do to change minds, the average voter must feel rather puny and ineffective. Thus, he organizes into the Tea Party and various other coolitions.

None of us regular folks can affect lawmakers like Big-Farming, Big-Pharma, Big-Medicine, Big-Unions, Big Military, Big Israel lovers, Big Military Manufacuring, and other huge money organizations.

Lawmakers are extremely vulnerable and sensitive to playing politics with public property. All it has taken in the past is a little insider information from a lobbyist, for example, to make millionaires of them because the pols can swoop in before the public is aware of a new building, bridge or road and buy up nearby land that will be worth millions before long.

Strange, isn't it? Our lawmakers seem to vote for things about which they care the most. Since money talks, a lobbyist's power is greater than a vote and that just doesn't seem right to me. Each time a lobbyist "bribes" a lawmaker, it depreciates the value of influence from all other sources and in my mind, we need to rid ourselves of influence peddling, however hard that goal may be. Those things make each of our votes less valuable.

I do not retreat from my position that as soon as possible we should eliminate the power of money politics from lobbyists. But even in a semi-free country, one with liberal judges, it is very difficult to take the bribe money out of Washington D.C politics because whenever the subject of lobbyists and money are litigated our liberal judges who for all intents and purposes have strayed from the Constitution become strict constructionists.

It used to be that you couldn't bribe Congress and then that changed. Now we have to wonder about our judiciary, even the liberal members of the Supreme Court. None, it seems, is above reproach.

We should instigate a test to all who presume to represent us, and I don't make distinctions. The Court, The Congress, and every member of the Administrative Branch including the non-approved, executive-appointed czars should be made to pass a test to determine if they can tell right from wrong. It would determine their moral terpetude? I think if we set loose some computer wizes they could come up with the proper questions and grading system.

Those that fail the "morals test" would be unfit to serve us and would be immediately disqualified. Those currently serving would have to take the test and if they failed, they, too, would be sent home to become janitors, insurance salesmen, benefit package presidents, or whatever they were doing before coming to Washington D.C. I dare say the swamp would be drained quickly and we would have to lower the age eligibility rules upon finding that only children were morally fit to serve.

An apostle of the Lord, Elder Quentin L. Cook, felt so strongly about how we in America and elsewhere are losing our moral compas that he had this to say at the April, 2012 General Conference of the Church of Jesus Christ of Latter-day Saints: "Freedom and light have never been easy to attain or maintain. Since the War in Heaven, the forces of evil have used every means possible to destroy agency and extinguish light. The assault on moral principles and religious freedom has never been stronger."

And don't tell me that some court somewhere would overrule it because it was morality was determined by a machine.

The George Bush doctrine of preemptive war is morally wrong. Under Don White's morality test, I doubt George W. Or his father would ever see the Oval Office. Double that for Barak Obama.

Our love of pre-emptive wars are immoral. If you consider scripture from God, which I do, I suggest you merely read either the Book of Mormon or the Bible for confirmation regarding how wicked this practice is. In my religion, God has sanctioned only wars of defense. Jesus Christ gave us the ultimate commandment and said that if our brother smites us, we should turn the check...

Wars of aggression, pre-emptive wars and pre-emptive strikes by remote-controlled aircraft called drones have stirred up a hornet's nest of anger toward the United States during the Bush and Obama administrations, which may explain the increase in terrorism around the world as suggested by Anup Shah in a Global Issues.com article of April 24, 2012.

Consider Mosiah, 29 in the Book of Mormon:

35 And he also unfolded unto them all the disadvantages they labored under, by having an unrighteous [a]king to rule over them;

36 Yea, all [a]his iniquities and abominations, and all the wars, and contentions, and bloodshed, and the stealing, and the plundering, and the committing of whoredoms, and all manner of iniquities which cannot be enumerated—telling them that these things ought not to be, that they were expressly repugnant to the commandments of God.

Gunboat diplomacy is not acceptable by conservatives and by civilized nations. But apparently it is okay by neo-con's, democrat's, and by progressive standards.

True conservatives do not run their foreign policy in this fashion. Those who approve of this kind of warfare are not conservatives. Therefore, Romney, Obama, Gingrich, and Santorum—the big war hawks of the elections—are definitely not military conservatives, but extremely liberal and even reckless.

When a nation like the United States gets so large and menacing to other nations, imagine what kind of intimidation power it possesses against its own citizens. The National Defense Appropriations Act (NDAA) doesn't ease the worry because therein is found language authorizing the unwarranted, impulsive, surreptitious arrest of America citizens and the non-constitutional transporting of them from their homes without due process, shipping or flying them to anywhere in the world to be unjustly thrown into a US government or clandestine foreign government jail for an interminable length of time without as little as telling them the charges with which they are being held.

Tis gorilla warfare, patriots. And they—our government—would have us believe that we have lost all semblance of Constitutional law because they said we are at war. If so, when does that so-called war end?Maybe never. That means our rights are also gone forever.

The Constitution says government's chief job is to protect our liberties. Those who choose security over liberty will soon lose both.

If ever you wanted to shout and demonstrate, now would be a very good time, except for one small detail. That Washington land—which you paid for in taxes — is now off limits to you who actually own the land. This is a classic case of the dog wagging the man, aka the formerly "free" citizen. Congress and a cynical president are both scared of their shadows. King George was also very much in fear of his life. That is one reason he put so many restrictions on his non-landed serfs.

It is the same in America today. Obama and his kind are afraid of what might happen to them if the people learn the truth—that he is a communist, a Muslim, and has aspirations, along with his progressive friends, to be the biggest dictators in the world. It is they, when congress fell asleep, who empowered the dog that is wagging all of our tails. Everything's haywire and backwards. The way they have things rigged, we the owners of government now must bend the knee to the whip of tyranny and bow down to these swine that yield the almighty vote in Congress. We once called them government servants, but while we watched they changed their names to government masters. Power corrupts. They are so corrupt that they feel it is us that must protect them?

We can no longer walk on that land near the White House and Capitol that we bought. We cannot demonstrate our disgust there. The question now is how can we expel that president and that congress without getting thrown in jail?

Vote them out of office in November. I won't stand for this and you shouldn't either, regardless of party affiliation. Both political parties are corrupt.

It's told in a little discussion I had with one of my neighbors:

"You said we can't go on certain government property?" he said.

"Yes, I said government property."

But I thought we bought that land with our tax dollars?" If so, we own it and no one, not even our president, can push us around like this."

"We did buy it, but now Washington—GOP and Democrats alike—feel their lives may be in danger and won't let us even get on the White House Lawn and other similar places." What big cowards they are!

"Their lives? What about my rights?" In the early years of our founding, patriots were willing to give their lives up to protect the country's liberty. What have we got for lawmakers today, a bunch of ninnyhammers?"

"Well, my answer to that is we must tell these sissies to "join the club. While we, the owners of that 'property' are having our rights truncated and threats made to our bodies and to our peace and tranquility, where is the government that is supposed to protect our liberties? Under the Constitution that was their chief job."

We're talking about our liberty—the one and only thing government is supposed to protect? They're our servants, not the other way around. And they tell us their main concern is *their* safety? Rubbish. They say that while turning on us with these crazy laws that remove our rights so that some invader, our own military, or even INTERPOL, an international law enforcement group, can carry us away to jail without so much as an attorney, a trial, charges read to us—you know all of our habeas corpus rights. Gone in a flash. Our own lawmakers have turned on us. They are tyrants and traitors, that's what they are and I won't stand for it. Even the privacy of our homes can be violated and we have no recourse? It's time to vote all of them out of office.

"First, we're intimidated by telling us we can't be on government sod, then they turn on us and say their agents can come into our houses unannounced and take us away in the dark of night to only God knows where? I can't believe this is America anymore. Can you? I can't stand this kind of cradle to grave treatment."

The things our own government can now do to us are awful. But there is more. Two years ago Obama signed an executive order allowing other nations through INTERPOL to come to our homes, taking you and I away without due process.

Read more on .com in a March first, 2012 article about how international cops now can arrest you at home, seize you and your family, and carry you away without recourse of the Fourth Amendment. Our rights are gone, that is unless we elect someone who cares more about our rights than about this myth of a war on terrorism. I have only heard Ron Paul, of all the candidates, complain about these things. He is the only one even vaguely aware that we've lost our rights. If the others know, they are too timid to talk publicly about it and you won't be able to count on them anyway.

Here's part of the article:

A little-discussed executive order from President Obama giving foreign cops new police powers in the United States by exempting them from such drudgery as compliance with the Freedom of Information Act is raising alarm among commentators who say INTERPOL already had most of the same privileges as diplomats.

"At David Horowitz's Newsreal Michael van der Galien said the issue is Obama's expansion of President Ronald Reagan's order from 1983 that originally granted those diplomatic privileges."

But, here's the difference: Reagan's order carried important exemptions requiring that INTERPOL to be subject to several U.S. laws to protect

Americans, such as the right to being represented by your choice of legal counsel and all the other habeas corpus rights we once enjoyed."

Are Tea Party Members True Patriots? True Conservatives?

Consider this irrefutable fact: Fortunately, it is true that many loyal Tea Party members are some of the most decorated and courageous veterans of foreign wars you will ever find—patriots—that is, people who observed their duty when called, happy to defend the American flag—and to even give their life for it if necessary defending liberty whenever and wherever the battle for Americans' freedom is waged.

They are not monolythic. Many of them are not conservatives—when you consider what it takes to be a patriot and a true conservative. A patriot is one who loves liberty, the Constitution, and what the Founders stood for and will fight to preserve liberty, even at the peril of his life in foreign wars if necessary. On the other hand, a conservative is a person living in America, here at home, who will fight in lawful ways with progressives and others to preserve his property, his life, and his rights under the Constitution.

Liberty is the essence of a true conservative. Patriotic true conservatives will accept the call of duty during Congressionally-declared and authorized wartime and fight valiantly. But, personal liberty is the bottom line—it's what we fight for. We don't go to war and come home victorious to preserve the rights of presidents and representatives in Washington to take our liberty away, piece by piece, through legislation and executive order. That's the role of a coward, not a conservative patriot.

Government is supposed to protect life, liberty, property, and the rights enumerated and those not enumerated. The inalienable rights given us from God are even more important than those noted in the Constitution and the Bill of Rights: life, liberty, and the pursuit of property—now changed to say the pursuit of happiness. The country can't be free if its people are living in fear of their government. This is what drove the Puritans from Holland and England to come to America in the first place.

Many Tea Party members were patriots of foreign wars, but here at home many of them have fallen asleep and seem to value security over liberty. They have become pussy cats regarding their own personal freedoms despite the fact that some of them are very visible and will show up in large numbers at political meetings and rallies under the lens of national TV.

Let us be clear—if you love Bush and Obama you love preemptive wars of aggression. These are wars that are not voted on or approved by Congress, wars which violate the spirit of America's founding. They include bombing and killing of innocent citizens of America and innocent people of other nations. If you find yourself on the side of the war hawks and "preventive wars" of aggression, you may not be a patriot at all or even a conservative.

There have been too many senseless wars, the Iraq and Afghanistan battles for example that have cost us more than $4 trillion dollars over the past ten years. It just isn't conservative at all to spend that kind of money on the basis of Madison Avenue-like propaganda claiming that we are now safer. Baloney! We are merely more hated across the globe, not safer.

You can't have personal freedom with a president like George Bush signing into law a so-called Patroit Act which essentially removed your rights while travelimg— your right of privacy and your right to move around the country peacefully without being accused of being a terrorist. You are also aware of laws which require the National Security Agency (NSA) to keep tabs on your every phone call, your every movement, every credit card purchase, and your likes and dislikes. The NSA and the others of the 16 government intelligence-gathering agencies of the U.S. government know more about you than you probably know about yourself.

Neither the Patriot Act or Obama's National Defense Authorization Act (NDAA) are to your benefit. Sure, NDAA funded our military. Which congressman from either party would deny our troops their pay and the best equipment money can buy? But the government is crafty. In addition to the pay part of the bill, they slipped in these other things that hatchet away at your Bill of Rights freedoms.

Military men and women volunteered to serve during peacetime and then some egotistical president caused a war undermined with questionable motives. Or haven't you heard? Most wars these days are contrived—the poking of our nose into someone else's business, carrying out a UN mandate (again, without Congressional approval), making of the US military the police force of the world at our unborn grandchildren's expense because US wars come at great cost and more and more wounded warriors means more cost to the Veteran's Administration and a less productive people.

As veterans of foreign wars, these fine people grew older and naturally they support the military. Soon, they themselves are war hawks.

We now can say very few Tea Party members are true conservatives. Neither is Mitt Romney, Rick Santorum, or Newt Gingrich. That shouldn't come as a big surprise to Tea Party people, our honored heroes of foreign wars. But we're not just making simple distinctions on paper. It is very important because true conservatives don't go to war unless our country is attacked. Let the sophists make the clever distinctions and war definitions. The fiction that we are constantly under attack by terrorists is government propaganda, a cover for their illicit wars lacking congressional-approval.

These wars are activities which both Bush and Obama have approved, but that doesn't make them right or legal. If it does, the office of president is far more powerful than the Founders anticipated. Congress was to have been the more powerful branch of government. *Now can you support Ron Paul?*

Congressman Paul was the only GOP guy running who served in the military? Yes, and for sure, the author of this book is biased, but Don White also served in the military. Barry Goldwater's "bomb-the-hell out-of-them" diplomacy was also not mine or Ron Paul's. It wasn't a true conservative stance, though many who thought they were conservatives got all pumped up about it.

Preemptive war is today's popular rhetoric among Tea Party people. In this way, many democrats who disdain warfare and prefer negotiations are far more conservative than many GOP hawks who tout war, and the threat of war, as one of America's chief weapons in this nation's arsenal of diplomatic options. What a horrible stance that is!

Ron Paul will eliminate the deficit in four years, saving a trillion dollars his first year, closely examining all foreign aid and probably getting rid of most or all of it since it is the cause of friction among nations living in the vicinity of those "chosen" nations receiving such aid. Foreign aid has never been proven to persuade other nations to like us. You can't buy friends in the world.

It is important to note that the BRIC nations of Brazil, Russia, India, and China—roughly half of the world's population—have recently chosen against America. They have noticed how shaky the dollar is, how this country has not paid off its debts and can not pay them, and they want out.

Can you blame them for wanting to have nothing to do with us, which is further support for my thesis that you can't buy true friends on this planet.

Deep down, Israel and other "allies" must hate us. Just as in our day-to-day relationships with other people, we choose to be friends with those who are most like us and from whom we benefit by being friends. Most of us would be highly offended if a friend tried to buy our loyalty with money. That is also true in foreign relations, but Washington has yet to get the message.

The point?

How can we best move America off this large rock on which it is Moored?

The only way is to completely clean house. The Democratic and Republican leadership is corrupt, acting in collusion with a corrupt president. Except for Mitt Romney and Ron Paul, the GOP candidates have been lackluster. Gingrich's so-called "Big Ideas," including his Moon Colony, are farcical. So are his other big spending agendas. Santorum's social agenda was all he had. The Evangelicals in the South fell for it, but then they also didn't approve of Paul and Romney. Strange, when you consider that these two men are the most religious men running. In a reprehensible way, the Evangelicals once again proved unreliable bell weathers of America sentament—as a whole. Santorum's big spending habits as a senator speak volumes about what damage this man would have done in the White House.

Obama's Stash Signals Danger

A preoccupation by many democrats in President Obama's supposed "stash" is dangerous. It is a reference to hate and envy, welfare, and class warfare/ This is what attracts his constituency to him. They don't have a clue as to his sinister side or about his platform because it changes from day to day. For them, all they need to know is that he gives hard-earned tax payer money away and they're on his list.

Deep down, Israel and other "allies" must dislike us immensely. Just as in our day-to-day relationships with other people, we choose to be friends with those by really being friends. Most of us would be highly offended if a friend tried to buy our loyalty with money. That is so true in foreign relations, but Washington has yet to get the message.

The point?

Again, how can we best move America off this large rock on which it is Moored?

Gingrich feins hating Romney, supposedly driving Newt on to the Tampa Convention and an open convention. But what was his real motivation to remain in the GOP presidential race? It was money-grubbing. He lost his only source of money when intrnational casino owner Sheldon Adelson, his big PAC donor, saw what a terrible campaigner he was. Gingrich considered this campaign a public-paid book tour. *How many books can I sell off an unsuspecting public?* He asked privately. He was also selling his name and photo for fifty bucks. No, Newt was not a sincere broker of good will. He was an entrepreuner who saw a campaign coming that he could glom onto for profit. It's all made up stuff—that story that he hates Romney. If Romney wins, Newt will be the first in line for a kushy government job, but if I were Mitt I would dismiss Gingrich for what he is, (as I said) a money-grubbing historian not fit for office.

Before he dropped out of the race, Santorum's social ideas of church and of falling in love with his wife and children again caught on. It was nice and most admirable, but his big spending habits as a senator spoke volumes about what damage this man would do in Washington.

Let Hate And Envy Thrive," Was Obama's Secret Mantra

A preoccupation by many democrats in President Obama's supposed "stash" is dangerous. It is a reference to hate and envy, welfare, class warfare—exactly what attracts his constituency to him. They don't have a clue as to his sinister side or about his platform. For them, all they need to know is that he gives our money away and they're on his list.

What else is there?

Obama is the great divider, not what he promised, bringing people together. Class warfare is his plan and it seems to be working out just about as he intended. For example, there's his dystopian notion that he conveyed to Joe The Plumber about spreading the wealth around the world and leveling America with the implication that he would sink America to about the same economic level as Kenya? He didn't use the word, Kenya, but you can bet it was on his mind. Many birthers still believe that is where he was born.

In some ways, Mr. Obama has already leveled the US, including what Heritage Foundation said about our now being in ninth place behind Canada as the "most" free nation on earth. But Obama's followers don't care about that abstract word "freedom." They don't take a longing for anything except the money he distributes to them. But if you think our "leveled" economy is bad now, wait a while. Inflation will soar along with jobless numbers. Already we've seen a 50 percent spike in food prices since he came to office and a two hundred percent jump in gas prices.

Yet Barak Obama sits there content in the White House doing nothing, approving very few new oil pumping sites and disapproving the Keystone pipeline from Canada—scornfully so, it seems, as he approved the pipeline leg from Oklahoma to Louisiana, knowing people would be fed up with his lack of compassion on the family that still drives a big vehicle because they have a lot of kids to take to school each day. Traditional families aren't his forte these days. He's now into the gay movement with which many believe he has numbered himself from the start. Obama's only advice to Americans tired of four-dollar gas is that it soon will go to five dollars. Fill your tires extra full, he says. And that man wants to lay this on us for another four years. No, absolutely, not!

Here's What Is Really Scary

To his moochers and sponges this man Obama is a living legend, but to most of us he is some kind of fictitious Robin Hood villain, taking from the rich to give to the poor; or is he a Satan worshiper, spreading temporary and false joy and happiness and money to all his friends? Of course the money isn't his, it was filched from hardworking American taxpayers.

Unprecedented In American Welfare Politics

Move over Lyndon Johnson and FDR. America has seen the light. We saw how by executive order Obama extended the length of unemployment benefits to 99 week, and that's almost two years that people can sit around drawing checks for doing almost nothing.

Lazy people are in love with the president's "big stash" and all the rest of his giveaway programs and ideas that slither across his silver tongue, past his big-teeth and out of his sinister-smiling mouth. That's what smoking did for him. It wrinkled his skin and destroyed his youthful appearance. But his biggest problem is his smoking, it's Obama's dangerous dance with the devil and the resulting loss and lack of sensitivity about right versus wrong. The man has no concept about lasting reality, truth and substance.

It doesn't really matter to his fans. "Give me mine while it's free and while he's here" is their mantra. But the more he hands out the "free" dollars to people, the bigger our problem becomes as American taxpayers and the longer the delay for America's day of reckoning.

This election year, 2012, everything is on the table, but really, it should be about one topic: saving America—not play-acting Santa Claus and electing a total failure of a president to a second term that he doesn't deserve. I predict that if we do re-elect this man, it will display to the world that we really don't care about our horrendous money problems and rating agencies will go wild, downgrading our currency once more—and maybe the last time before the bottom falls out and there is no more American Dream. What will life be like when that happens here in the USA? When there is no more America, "land of the free?"

The stock market fears an Obama second term as much as true conservatives and the job market. Folks, don't believe a thing this man says. It can only get worse under an Obama second term and it will, count on it and get your food and staple storage there so that you will have something to eat when times really get tough.

Our liberty is at stake, but unfortunately the dumb and stupid in America have no idea of the magnitude of what we stand to lose if the GOP loses this election a second time to the son of two avowed communists. It should be pointed out that despite the fact that Barak Hussein Obama has said he is a Christian and believes in the free enterprise system, not communism, his actions tell us otherwise—he is really a Muslim lover and a purveyor of Marxist ideas in all he does.

A conservative American must become president this time around—because America is terminally ill and needs and deserves saving and it can't be done by someone who carries the disease of a New World Order and dystopian ideas in his head that caused the problem in the first place. America is afflicted with a deep financial illness, and the red alert hospital room lights and shrill sound will soon sound noting a critically ill country is about to expire. Only a doctor conservative, an honest man sitting in the White House, can resuscitate and cure the virus in the patient this time, all man made—brought about by Keynesian thinking and progressives in Washington.

We need someone who understands the financial world and its instability and the remedy that can save us from this deep monetary virus that bad men have thrown into the path of a big-hearted country. If something isn't done soon, America will see the collapse of the dollar and massive inflation, resulting in a second Great Depression—all caused by the Time Bomb: *America's $20-Trillion Nightmare* that is about to go off in our face. This is the name of a forthcoming book by Don white.

This cataclysmic money problem is causing instability that will soon destroy us as a nation if we are not careful. Take a look at Greece if you don't believe that. They are bartering for food, giving up cigarettes and any gold they possess for bread. We must act fast, decisively, and purposefully to save our glorious nation, America.

The bottom line is that Dr. Ron Paul is the only strategically positioned man qualified to save us. He will reduce government size and straighten things out in Washington by merely being Ron Paul, Mr. conservative; and by following his own plan. It is to save trillions of dollars right away by cutting five departments of the executive branch including Education and Welfare, sending those duties back to the states, bringing our troops home, and ending the Fed.

But the biggest piece of the puzzle of saving America could be the printing of our own interest-free, debt-free money which we should call Greenbacks after Lincolns successful printing America's own money to pay for the Civil War and for saving the Union.

We can print our own debt-free, interest-free money that will allow us to pay off our mounting debt.

Saving America—An Impossible Dream? Not At All, Just Vote For Paul

Dr. Ron Paul would downsize government, balance the budget, save trillions of dollars and pay off our national debt in four years, preserving the integrity of a great nation. Is that an impossible dream? Not at all. Just vote for Paul—and tell your friends to do likewise—and watch this impossible dream unfold. The phony baloney talk from other candidates is cheap and insincere. But you need to know that Ron Paul's plan is so simple and straightforward and conservative that the charlatans who run our Treasury and the Federal Reserve couldn't think of it in a million years because their brains are too clouded with deceit and chicanery. When a Ron Paul comes along, a truly honest conservative, it scares them to death. Simple truth always frightens those who operate in dark, secret shadows. The One World sophists are worried because Paul's brilliant ideas could blow away their plans for world domination. It ruins everything they have ever planned for this planet since Rothschild took control of European banks and worldwide monetary affairs, knowing that whoever controls the amount of money printed and interest rates is master of the world.

The tragedy is that so few Americans bother to find out what Ron Paul stands for. I wrote the summary version of *Liberty Defined*, called *Patriot Call of Ron Paul*, to help remedy that. It has been available for three months as an e-book at amazon.com and

Barnes & Noble. Now you can read the paperback version, too.

I was tempted to call my book *Liberty Defined For Dummies* but that title has too many negative connotations and those who read and accept it are the most intelligent Americans around, not dummies. That is why I called the book *Patriot's Call of Ron Paul.* There are two volumes published in e-book format, but all 50 of Ron Paul's essential issues, principles and imperatives for freedom are *included in this new soft-cover print volume.*

Liberty Defined is Paul's eighth book, a New York Times best seller. What other current Congressman has written so well, so prolifically? My book is a take-off from that. I also whole-heartedly endorse Congressman Paul's other books that I have read, especially *End the Fed.*

According to an eminent University of Georgia political scientist Keith Poole, since 1937 Ron Paul has had the most conservative voting record of any member of Congress. His son Rand Paul was elected to theUS Senate from Kentucky in 2011, making the elder Paul the first Representative in history to serve concurrently with his son, and vice versa. Thanks to the Pauls, the country's attention has turned toward auditing—then ending—the Federal Reserve.

Disclaimers

The author of this book disclaims any and all liability for omissions or errors found in the book, and for any content or comments that may be alleged libelous.

Don White is not the originator of most issues and ideas for the book. They are Ron Paul's. I just happen to share most of his ideas, but he didn't put me up to it. I did write my version of the book's fifty principles and added material for clarity sake and to bring the reader up-to-date with new damaging legislation that has been signed by Obama in the last six months, something you will not find in Paul's books.

I want to do everything I can to attract students of voting age to read this book. I want them to begin to understand the Constitution and how Ron Paul reads politics. He is right, of course. The liberal professors and pols are wrong.

My words are in the book, But I have lavished onto the pages many quotations, direct and indirect, from Mr. Paul. In this way the book, *Patriot Call Of Ron Paul*, represents a short version of Ron

Paul's book in issues, chapter organization and content.

Thanks to **Marcus White** who wrote and formatted the cover and assisted me in editing this book.

I'll warn you: the opinions expressed in the book are factual but hard-hitting. They are not all, but virtually all, Ron Paul's. I agree with him in all cases except when he gets into legalizing drugs and allowing Iran nukes. He is consistent in every way, nations should not try to exert their will over other countries unless to defend themselves. Preemptive wars of aggression, anticipating that nation will attack you, are not acceptable.

As one world order, a world run by the distant elites, is not the answer to anything because it would lead to money domination by the Rothschilds and the central banks that he controls. It would do just as Obama has said—the entire world would become poor and good old American genius, ingenuity, and inventiveness would cease. Removing government from the local people has never worked in America; and creating a super central government is a bad idea because it would take government further away from the people who count. The average American wouldn't stand a chance.

Ron Paul is an excellent writer. In fact, I like his written word much better than his spoken word. My family and I support Mr. Paul over and above all of the other candidates. For religious affinity only, it would be logical for me to have supported two other primary candidates.

I felt that *Patriot Call Of Ron Paul* would be beneficial to his campaign. I want more people reading and becoming converted to his excellent ideas. My guess is that millions of people already agree with these ideas, but no one but Paul has come long to champion them…though it's already almost May, 2012, Patriot Call could still help to accomplish this. My Patriot e-book and this paperback edition are priced conservatively and are affordable for most readers. The e-book is only $2.99 per volume (2 volumes) at Barnes and Noble and Amazon.com   http://bit.ly/tjGsUc

Unfortunately for Mr. Paul and for America, our country has changed from a freedom loving, free enterprise nation with middle-class prosperity to one with a block of youth and middle and low income voters who, because they are welfare recipients or have been on the public dole or know someone who is, can't see anything wrong with the direction Barak Obama has taken us. Through clouded lenses, sadly, some of them must feel that this president is best suited to bringing us out of our double-dip recession using failed Democrat voodoo stimulus concoctions.

Happily, however, many youths and former supporters of Obama of all age groups—a growing number—have deserted Obama, understanding that Keynesian economics is a bankrupt system. In 2012 Mr. Obama was so skittish about his new Keynesian-style jobs bill that he waited almost a month to file it with Congress. You can't blame him. It received heavy criticism both from sides of the isle because it would increase the deficit by at least two trillion dollars. Many believe he was merely using it as a campaign banner, a class warfare slogan to pit the "have-nots" against the "haves," hoping to garner a large block of undecided voters. Good luck with that—they're angry at you, sir.

Obama has changed politics in Washington. He has pushed America farther to the left than any previous president and further along the road of corruption and despair. He does things no previous president would even think of doing. I'm speaking about his blatant attempt to sway the Supreme Court by making a "presidential" visit to the Supreme Court ostensibly to visit his old solicitor general Elena Kagan, but with the purpose of making it a television media event out of it to put pressure on the Supreme Court.

This is a despicable act of treason and should not be tolerated by a John Boehner and Harry Reid Congress that too often looks the other way. It should should roundly censor him or even start impeachment proceedings. This president is scared to death and is reacting like a mad man. He's unstable and unfit to govern from the White House. He knows he's going to lose this election and realizes things can't get worse so why not chance impeachment if it will help him win.

Washington bureaucrats are too close to the action to gage the will of the people. In many American minds the Obama regressive and frankly twisted and evil attitude about welfare and liberty has created for Ron Paul and for the entire Republican Party an opportunity, though it be a steep constituency educational curve to overcome. Romney, Paul and the GOP must defeat false ideas found in the minds and hearts of these democratic-leaning Americans.

I predict there will yet be a groundswell of enthusiasm for Ron Paul even among democrats. He has already placed second and third in many primaries and caucuses. Overall, Paul was in second place among four Republican contenders in delegate count as of March 1, 2012, just before the Michigan and Arizona primaries. He could do even better as time goes on. Many democrats are conservative about causing wars. So is Paul. Many want to tone down the spending and pay off the debt that, frankly, threatens to end our independence. That's Paul's agenda.

The big bankers who own the media told their underlings to ignore Ron Paul, don't give him any press. They tell the press to report Paul's numbers are so low that he can't possibly win. All of this is propaganda, for he has the heart of the people with him.

Scurrilous journalists would now lie, cheat and intentionally take tapes of people apart just to prove their side of an argument. NBC has been proven to be such a group of unreliable scumbags, as evidenced in the Zimmerman shooting of the Trayvon Martin teenager. We the public do not know what to believe from these banker-controlled channels. Their so-called "journalists" may have once been honest but now they take orders from a media that is guided by the Bilderberg mob. They have disgraced themselves to profane levels just to keep their jobs, which is supposed to be reporting the truth.

Journalism is unrecognizable when compared to twenty years ago. It once was regarded as the noble Fourth Estate, a watchdog over corrupt government. Well, whose watch-dogging the corrupt media these days despite a scant few like Rush Limbaugh?

Both Republican and Democratic parties are operating in a scandalous manner. They learned with the Bush election in Florida that if they bribed the local delegates and leaders—or had them in their pockets, anyway—it wouldn't matter what the voters said in the voting booths. I am not a democrat, but a disgusted republican. I plan to write more about this national disgrace later.

At one time America had fair elections, unlike the rest of the world. Now it's America's elections in each state—especially during the primaries—that the UN's secretary general Kofi Annan needs to investigate, rather than another North African or South American third world state. He should be monitoring the U.S. for honesty, and he may find none.

I am reluctant to say that because it is diametrically contrary to what I believe America's independence should be all about. We should never have to bow to a foreign nation or to a corrupt United Nations. Unfortunately, our elections are often corrupt on both sides, democrats and republicans. We, the voters, need to be aware of that and join together to change it.

When someone says Ron Paul can't win, it isn't true. Just remember, the man who said that is a neoconservative himself, someone who isn't concerned about America's financial future. Tell him he is dead wrong.

I yet hope to see a large number of other new books, articles, and spoken word endorsing Mr. Paul's ideas, publicly proclaiming him, as I have, as the one candidate who has the financial mind and ability to turn our economy around, reduce the size and influence of government, making America prosperous again.

Congressman Ron Paul

About The Author

Don White is a veteran journalist, a former Associated Press newsman who also writes fiction including a published suspense thriller and two on the way. *The Exterminato* is an e-book thriller that will soon appear in a new edition under the title *Murder By Executive Order.*

Besides authoring many short stories, His other fiction includes two novels currently underway, **The Hun**ted and **Civil War 2014.**

White owns and edits several websites in Orlando, Florida. One is http://prespaul.blogspot.com which he put up in 2011 to support congressman Ron Paul's bid for the Republican nomination for president. It will remain operational through the August GOP convention in Tampa, FL and beyond because it is chalk-full of articles, videos, and news not only about Ron Paul's election efforts, but his interesting and legitimate take on liberty and America's free enterprise system.

Everything Don White has written about Dr. Paul is based on moral, Christian standards and the US Constitution because of all candidates running for office, Paul follows the Constitution more closely and avidly. Paul and White are strict Constitutional constructionists.

Mr. White received his high school education at Granite High School in Salt Lake County and gained his undergraduate education at both Utah State University in Logan, Utah and the University of Utah in Salt Lake City. He took engineering and journalism courses, writing for the Daily Utah Chronicle while an undergraduate and assisting Utah Athletic Department Publicist Harry James. He lettered in baseball for three years under the late Pres Sumerhays, playing centerfield.

White served a 30-month mission for the Church of Jesus Christ of Latter-day Saints, acting as mission historian, traveling elder, branch president, and assistant editor of the Valkeus, the mission magazine. Later he assisted Bob Coles, editor of the *Utah Homeowner Magazine* and the Utah Contractor Magazine.

White holds three degrees or certificates, Bachelor of Science, U. of U.; Juris Doctor, Howard Taft University; and Chartered Property & Casualty Underwriter (CPCU) from the American Institutes.

He worked for several insurance companies, including The Hartford, Bear River Mutual, Transamerica in Salt Lake City, and Western National Mutual Insurance Group in Seattle and

Minneapolis. He was president/CEO for eight years for Western National which had offices in Minneapolis and Seattle. During that time he served on many insurance boards and committees and was chairman of the Minnesota Insurance Federation.

Don served as cub master, scout master, and little league coach in baseball and basketball for his three sons. He is married and he and his wife have four children

Don White

www.ingramcontent.com/pod-product-compliance
Lightning Source LLC
Chambersburg PA
CBHW060232290526
45789CB00001B/15